ABOUT CSS GRID EXPLAINI

CSS Grid is revolutionizing the fro...

For the last 20 years, web designers have used CSS to lay out web pages. However, CSS has always been missing some key functionality. Designers had to rely on workarounds, such as tables, floats, and positioning.

Isn't it crazy that our main layout tool was so reliant on hacks and misused features?

CSS Grid is different and better.

CSS Grid allows you to create a grid-based layout system, using columns and rows. You don't have to use any workarounds. You don't have to use different hacks for different browsers. You don't have to install any extra frameworks.

CSS Grid has been around since 2011, but has recently exploded in popularity. Almost all major browsers support CSS Grid. The only exceptions are Internet Explorer 11 and Opera Mini.

In this short book, you are going to master the key ideas behind CSS Grid.

In the first chapter, we start with the basic terminology. You'll learn the difference between Grid Areas and Grid Cells, between Grid Tracks and Grid Gaps.

Then, using a hands-on approach, you'll start building CSS Grids. There are nine different exercises in this book. You'll build everything from the most basic CSS Grid to a full site layout.

ABOUT THE OSTRAINING EVERYTHING CLUB

CSS Grid Explained is part of the OSTraining Everything Club.

The club gives you access to all of the video classes, plus all the "Explained" books from OSTraining.

- These books are always up-to-date. Because we self-publish, we can release constant updates.
- These books are active. We don't do long, boring explanations.
- You don't need any experience. The books are suitable even for complete beginners.

Join the OSTraining Everything Club today by visiting our website at https://ostraining.com. You'll be able to download ebook copies of "CSS Grid Explained" and all our other books and videos.

WE OFTEN UPDATE THIS BOOK

We aim to keep this book up-to-date, and so will regularly release new versions to keep up with changes in the CSS Grid specification. This is version 2.0 of CSS Grid and was released on June 10, 2019.

ADVANTAGES AND DISADVANTAGES

We often release updates for this book. Most of the time, frequent updates are wonderful. If there is a change in the CSS Grid in the morning, we can have a new version of this book available in the afternoon. Most traditional publishers wait years and years before updating their books.

There are two disadvantages to be aware of:

- Page numbers do change. We often add and remove material from the book to reflect changes in CSS Grid.
- There's no index at the back of this book. This is because page numbers do change, and also because our self-publishing platform doesn't have a way to create indexes yet. We hope to find a solution for that soon.

Hopefully, you think that the advantages outweigh the disadvantages. If you have any questions, we're always happy to chat: books@ostraining.com.

THANK YOU TO OUR READERS

If you find anything that is wrong or out-of-date, please email us at books@ostraining.com. We'll update the book, and to say thank you, we'll provide you with a new copy.

ARE YOU AN AUTHOR?

If you enjoy writing about the web, we'd love to talk with you.

Most publishing companies are slow, boring, inflexible and don't pay very well.

Here at OSTraining, we try to be different:

- **Fun**: We use modern publishing tools that make writing books as easy as blogging.
- **Fast**: We move quickly. Some books get written and published in less than a month.
- **Flexible**: It's easy to update your books. If technology changes in the morning, you can update your book by the afternoon.
- **Fair**: Profits from the books are shared 50/50 with the author.

Do you have a topic you'd love to write about? We publish books on almost all web-related topics.

Whether you want to write a short 100-page overview, or a comprehensive 500-page guide, we'd love to hear from you.

Contact us via email: books@ostraining.com.

ARE YOU A TEACHER?

We hope that many schools, colleges and organizations will adopt CSS Grid Explained as a teaching guide to CSS Grid.

This book is designed to be a step-by-step guide that students can follow at different speeds. The book can be used for a one-day class or a longer class over multiple weeks.

If you are interested in teaching CSS Grid, we'd be delighted to help you with review copies, and all the advice you need.

Please email books@ostraining.com to talk with us.

SPONSOR AN OSTRAINING BOOK

Is your company interested in sponsoring an OSTraining book? Our books are some of the world's best-selling guides to the software they cover. People love to read our books and learn about new web design topics.

Why not reach those people? Partner with us to showcase your company to thousands of web developers. We have partnered with Acquia, Pantheon, Nexcess, GoDaddy, InMotion, GlowHost and Ecwid to provide sponsored training to millions of people.

If you want to learn more, visit https://ostraining.com/sponsor or email us at books@ostraining.com.

WE WANT TO HEAR FROM YOU

Are you satisfied with your purchase of CSS Grid Explained? Let us know and help us reach others who would benefit from this book.

We encourage you to share your experience. Here are two ways you can help:

- Leave your review on Amazon's product page of CSS Grid Explained.
- Email your review to books@ostraining.com.

Thanks for reading CSS Grid Explained. We wish you the best in your future endeavors with the software!

THE LEGAL DETAILS

This book is Copyright © OSTraining.

This book is published by OSTraining.

Proper names and contact information are used as examples in this book. No association with any organization or individual is intended, nor should it be inferred.

CSS Grid Explained

CSS GRID EXPLAINED

Your Step-by-Step Guide to CSS Grid

JORGE MONTOYA AND STEVE BURGE

OSTraining

CSS Grid Explained Copyright © by OSTraining. All Rights Reserved.

CONTENTS

1. Introduction to CSS Grid Terminology — 1
2. Creating Your First CSS Grid — 6
3. Using the Firefox Grid Inspector — 12
4. How to Create Explicit and Implicit Grids — 19
5. How to Use the Autoflow Property in CSS Grid — 24
6. How to Use the FR Unit For Layouts — 32
7. How to Size Tracks with the Auto Keyword — 40
8. How to Size Grid Items with the Span Keyword — 47
9. How to Use Line Numbers in CSS Grid — 54
10. How to Layer Items In CSS Grid — 63
11. How to Use Line Names in CSS Grid — 72
12. How to Place Items with Grid Template Areas — 82
13. How to Use the minmax() Function — 90
14. How to Use the auto-fill and auto-fit Keywords — 99
15. The grid-auto-flow: dense Property — 108

16.	How to Align Items in CSS Grid	117
17.	The justify-content and align-content Properties	129
18.	How to Nest Grids	138

CHAPTER 1.

INTRODUCTION TO CSS GRID TERMINOLOGY

The basic concept of CSS Grid is to take an HTML element and divide it into rows and columns. This process will turn the HTML element into a grid that can be used for layouts.

Take a look at the image below. We'll use this code as our first CSS Grid example.

You can declare the wrapping `<div class="main">` as a grid. Then the `header` and `body` elements will be considered as grid items.

The `<h1>` and `<aside>` elements are inside grid items but will not become grid items themselves.

```
<div class="main">           ──▶ Grid container
    <header>       ──▶ Grid item
        <h1>First Grid Example</h1>    ──▶ Not a grid item
    </header>
    <body>
        <article>
            Lorem ipsum dolor sit amet consectetur adipisicing elit.
            Officiis laboriosam architecto amet distinctio nulla reiciendis,
            incidunt at iusto, doloremque excepturi cum placeat. Molestiae dolor
            ab quo eaque similique suscipit exercitationem error sint.
            Laudantium repudiandae aperiam aspernatur iure ipsam non ut quia nemo labore at
            eligendi, excepturi maxime praesentium error minima.
        </article>
    </body>
</div>
```

This is the fundamental concept behind CSS Grid: you can use normal HTML elements to create grids and layouts. You don't need any special frameworks.

In this chapter, I'm going to introduce you to six key terms we use in talking about CSS Grid.

#1. GRID LINE

The grid line is the most basic unit of the grid. Your grid layout is defined by your grid lines.

You can refer to lines by number, or you can even give them a custom name. As we'll see later in this book, custom names can be very useful when working with more complex layouts.

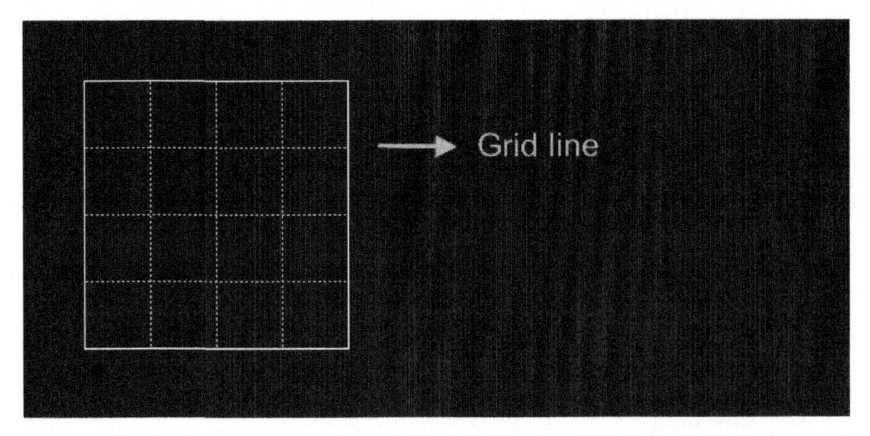

#2. GRID CONTAINER

The Grid Container is the wrapping element for all the grid items. You define a grid container with this single CSS property:

```
.main {
display: grid;
}
```

→ Grid container

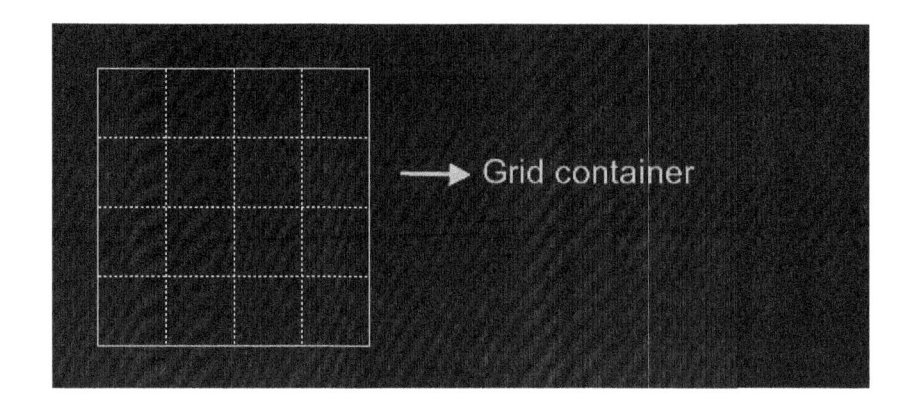

#3. GRID CELL

A Grid Cell is an area surrounded by four grid lines. You can think of a grid cell as being just like a spreadsheet cell.

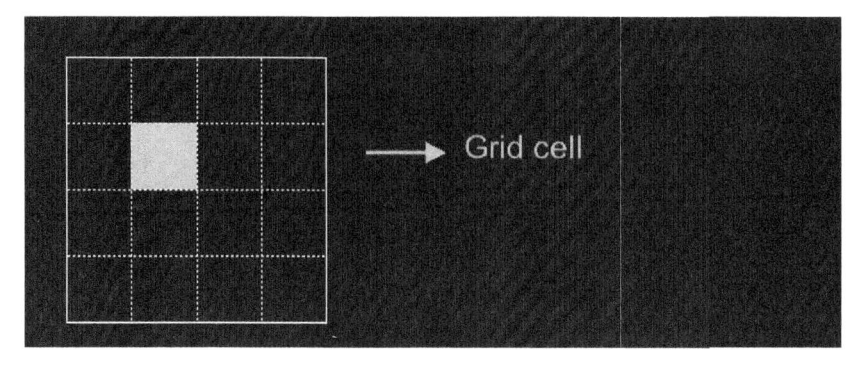

→ Grid cell

#4. GRID AREA

A Grid Area is composed of multiple grid cells.

The CSS Grid module currently allows you to define rectangular or square areas. But you won't be able to define more complex areas such as an L-shaped figure.

→ Grid Area

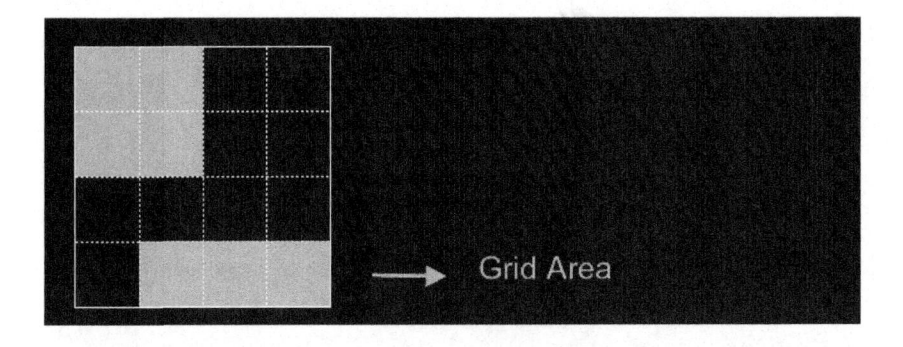

#5. GRID TRACK

Grid Track is a general term to identify rows or columns.

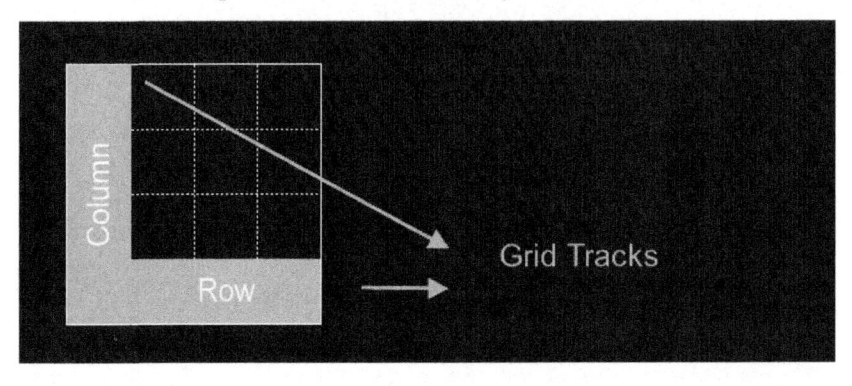

→ Grid Tracks

#6. GRID GAP

A Grid Gap is the space between grid cells or grid areas. You can think of it as being similar to the `margin` in HTML.

You cannot place content in a grid gap. By default the grid gap is 0, which means there is no separation between the cells in a grid.

The gap is defined with the CSS `grid-gap` property.

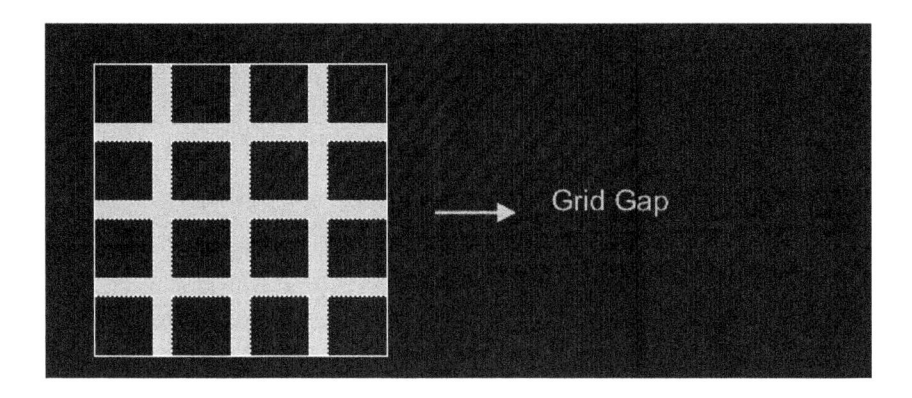

WHAT'S NEXT?

In this chapter, we introduced six key terms that you'll see throughout this book:

1. Grid Line
2. Grid Container
3. Grid Cell
4. Grid Area
5. Grid Track
6. Grid Gap

In the next chapter, we'll put that knowledge to use by creating our first CSS Grid.

CHAPTER 2.

CREATING YOUR FIRST CSS GRID

Now that you have learned the CSS Grid basics, it's time to build your first grid.

All the code in this book is available for download from our Github account: https://github.com/OSTraining/cssgrid. For example, the code for this chapter is located in the /css-grid/ folder: https://github.com/OSTraining/cssgrid/tree/master/css-grid.

Here's what our grid will look like:

- The grid will contain nine elements.
- Each one of these elements will be laid out in a 3×3 grid.
- Each column will have a width of 100px.
- The grid items will be separated from each other by a 20px gap.

WRITE THE HTML CODE

Let's write the HTML code for our grid.

- Create a folder called /css-grid/. We'll use this for all the files in this exercise.
- Create a file called css-grid.html inside the /css-grid/

folder.

- Open the file in a text editor.
- Write the following code:

```html
<html>

<head>
<link         rel="stylesheet"         type="text/css" href="css-grid.css">
</head>

<body>

<div class="container">
<div class="item">1</div>
<div class="item">2</div>
<div class="item">3</div>
<div class="item">4</div>
<div class="item">5</div>
<div class="item">6</div>
<div class="item">7</div>
<div class="item">8</div>
<div class="item">9</div>
</div>

</body>

</html>
```

As you can see, this HTML is relatively simple. The HTML for our grid is only a `div` containing nine other `div`s.

WRITE THE CSS CODE

Now let's write the CSS code for our grid.

- Create a file called css-grid.css in the same /css-grid/

folder.

- Open the css-grid.css file in a text editor.
- Write this code:

```css
/* GLOBAL STYLES */

* {
box-sizing: border-box;
}

body {
background-color: #AAA;
background-size: 340px, auto;
margin: 50px;
}

/* Each item in the grid contains numbers */
.item {

/* Center the contents of the grid items. Make each grid item a Flex Container */
display: flex;

/* Horizontal and Vertical centering */
justify-content: center;
align-items: center;
border: 5px solid #87b5ff;
border-radius: 3px;
font-size: 2em;
font-family: sans-serif;
font-weight: bold;
background-color: #1c57b5
}
```

- Save the css-grid.css file.
- Open the css-grid.html file in your browser. Your screen

will look like the image below:

Look back at the CSS and you'll see that every element inside the containing wrapper has been defined as a flex container, thanks to this code: `display: flex;`

Making every element into a flex container allows us to easily center the content horizontally and vertically.

CREATE THE GRID CONTAINER

In the last step, we created the CSS for each grid cell. Now it's time to declare the grid container.

- Add this code to your cssgrid.css file:

```
.container {
display: grid;
}
```

This code turns the `div` with the class `container` into a grid container and all child items inside it into grid items.

If you take a look at your browser, you won't see any changes yet.

This is because you have defined the grid container, but you haven't specified yet how the items inside that container will be placed.

- Add the following lines to your cssgrid.css code and save

the file:

```
.container {
display: grid;
grid-template-columns: 100px 100px 100px;
}
```

In this code, you just have explicitly defined three columns. The `grid-template-columns` property enables you to define the columns of the grid. Each one of these three columns will have a width of 100px.

- Refresh the css-grid.html file in your browser. Your screen will now look like the image below:

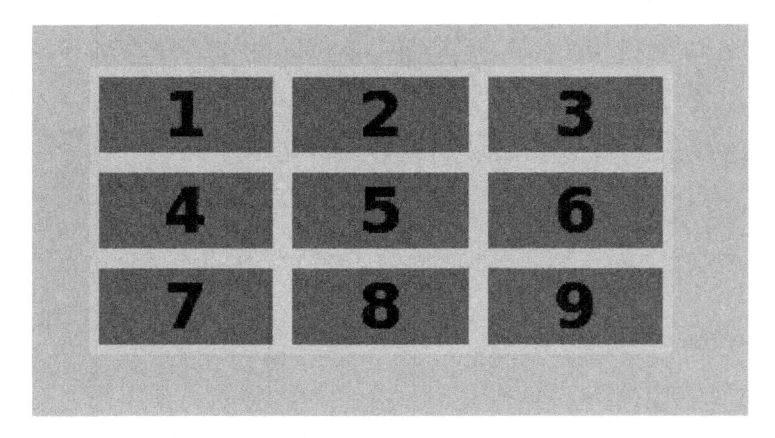

Look back at the CSS code you just wrote. Notice that you didn't define the number of rows in the grid. These rows were added in an implicit way by the browser.

If you define the columns or rows in a grid, it's called an "Explicit Grid". On the other hand, if the grid items are placed automatically by the browser, it's called an "Implicit Grid".

SEPARATE THE GRID ITEMS

Looking at our current CSS Grid, you'll notice that there is no separation between the grid items.

You can add separation using the `grid-column-gap` and `grid-row-gap` properties.

There's also a a shorthand that integrates both properties: `grid-gap`. Let's add this to your current CSS file.

- Edit your cssgrid.css file and add grid-gap: 20px; to the .container. This is how the .container code will look with the extra line:

```
.container {
display: grid;
grid-template-columns: 100px 100px 100px;
grid-gap: 20px;
}
```

- Refresh your browser, and your css-grid.html display will look like this:

Congratulations! You just have created your first CSS Grid!

CHAPTER 3.

USING THE FIREFOX GRID INSPECTOR

In the first two chapters of this book, you learned the basics of CSS Grid.

In this chapter, we're going to dig a little deeper. We'll show you how to use the Grid Inspector tool in the Firefox browser. Firefox has several very useful tools for when you're working with CSS Grid.

THE GRID INSPECTOR IN FIREFOX

If you don't already have Firefox installed on your computer, go to https://mozilla.org.

- Open your css-grid.html file in Firefox.
- Open Firefox Dev Tools. You can do this using the Ctrl + Shift + I buttons in Windows/Linux or the Cmd + Opt + I button on a Mac.
- We're going to use the "Inspector" feature in Firefox Dev Tools, so make sure the Inspector tab is active.
- Click the grid container element. You can identify this element in the HTML pane with the word grid, as in the image below:

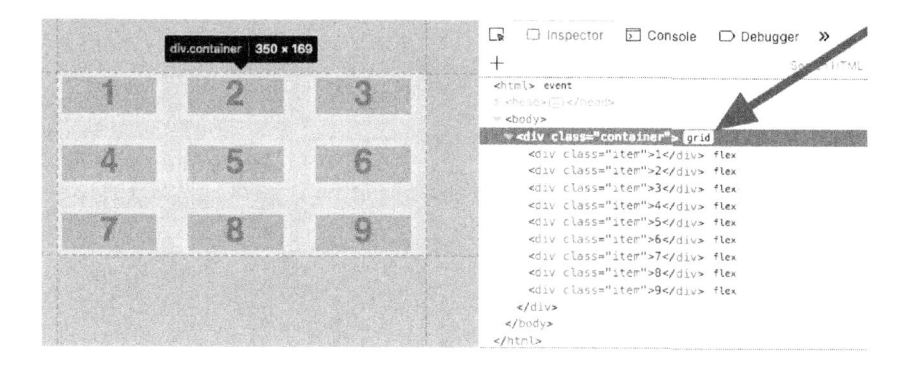

- Click the "Layout" tab in Firefox Dev Tools, as shown below:

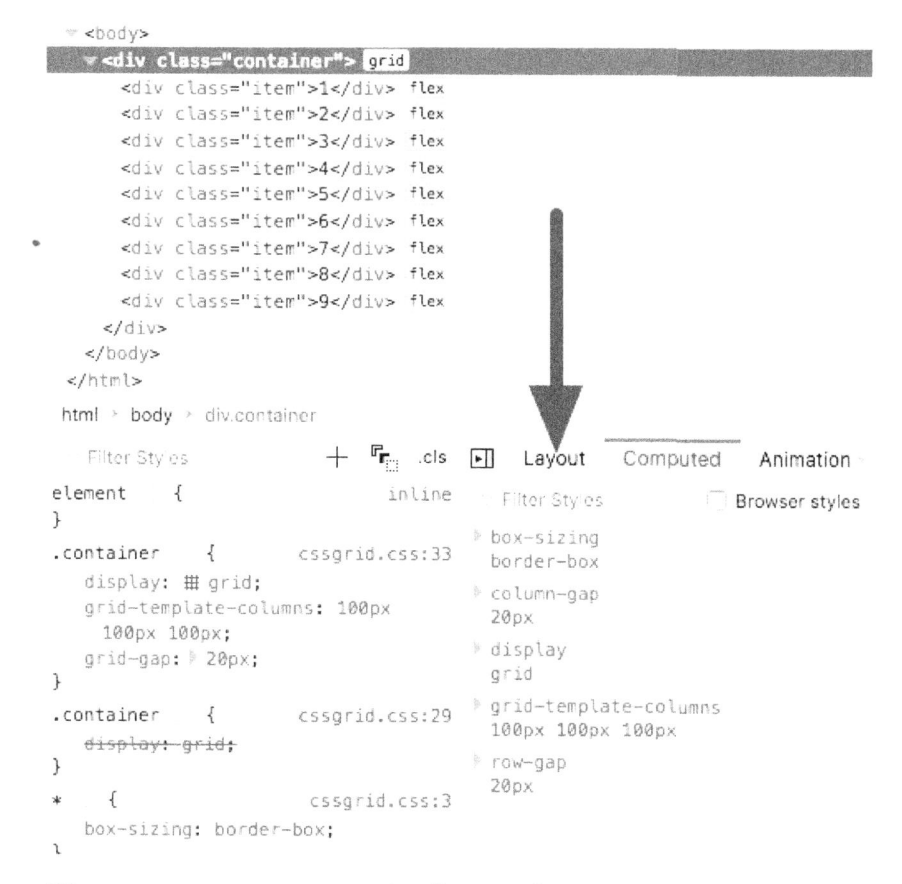

There are two sections in this "Layout" tab:

- Grid

CSS GRID EXPLAINED 13

- Box Model

```
html > body > div.container

  Filter       body              +    .cls    [▶]   Layout    Computed    Animation
element         {                        inline    ▶ Grid
}
.container       {         cssgrid.css:33          ▶ Box Model
  display: ▦ grid;
  grid-template-columns: 100px
    100px 100px;
  grid-gap: ▶ 20px;
}
.container       {         cssgrid.css:29
  display: grid;
}
*         {                 cssgrid.css:3
  box-sizing: border-box;
}
```

The "Grid" section contains settings you can use to control the display of the grid.

You can use the "div.container" checkbox in order to show or hide the grid container:

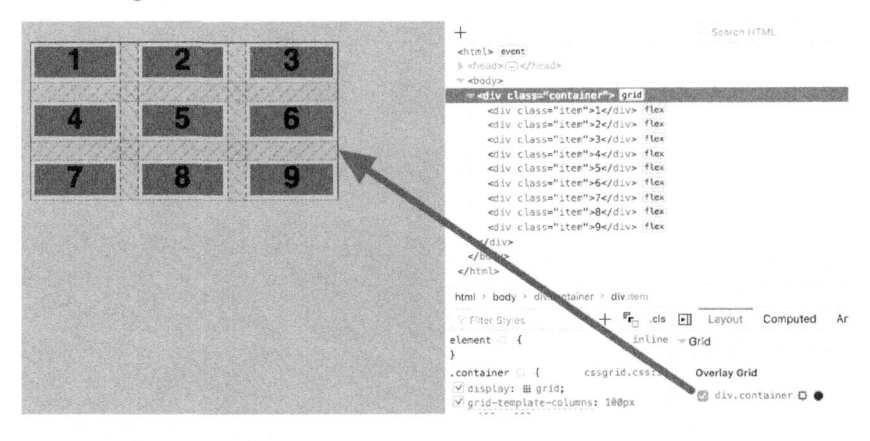

This grid display has a color switcher which lets you define the color of the grid. This is very useful when you have multiple grids in one page, or if the background color of your site is similar to the color of the grid.

14 JORGE MONTOYA AND STEVE BURGE

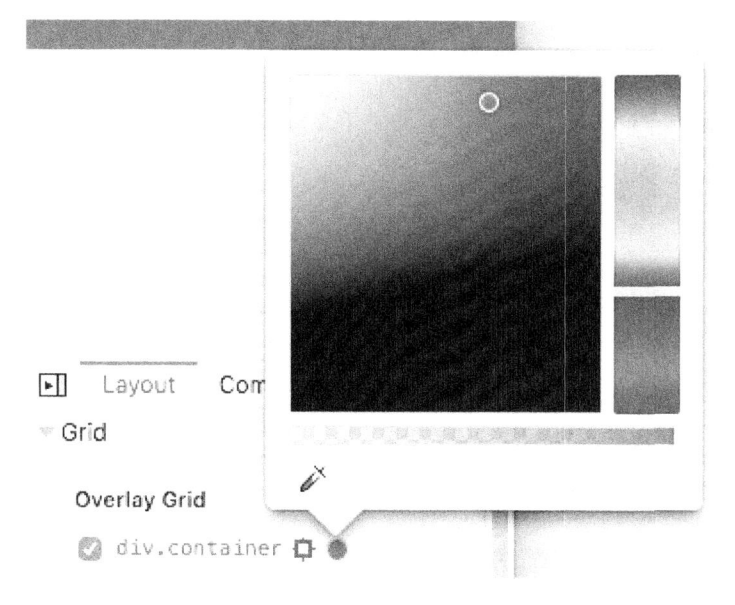

You see an option to "Display line numbers", which lets you configure the line numbers and their appearance.

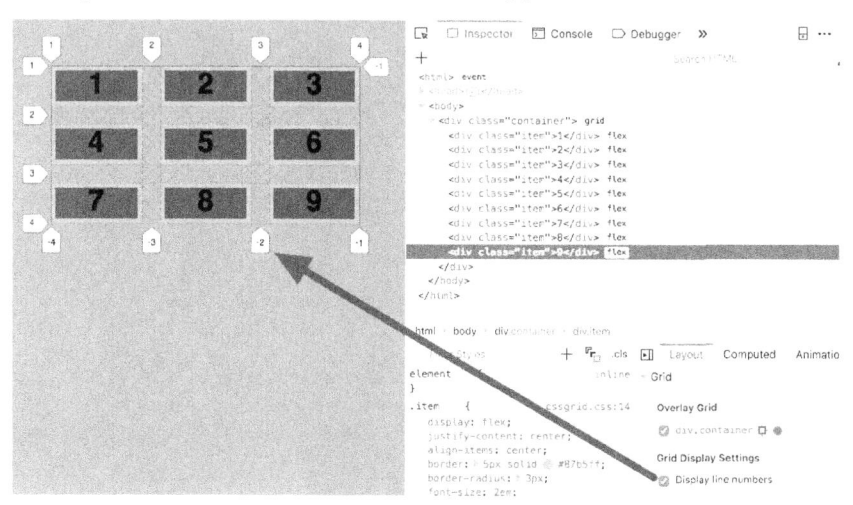

There is also an option to display the names of the declared areas inside the grid. However, we haven't declared any names yet, so this option won't do much at this moment.

The Mini Grid view lets you easily locate the position of a grid area. It provides information about the dimensions of the selected area and its position.

CSS GRID EXPLAINED 15

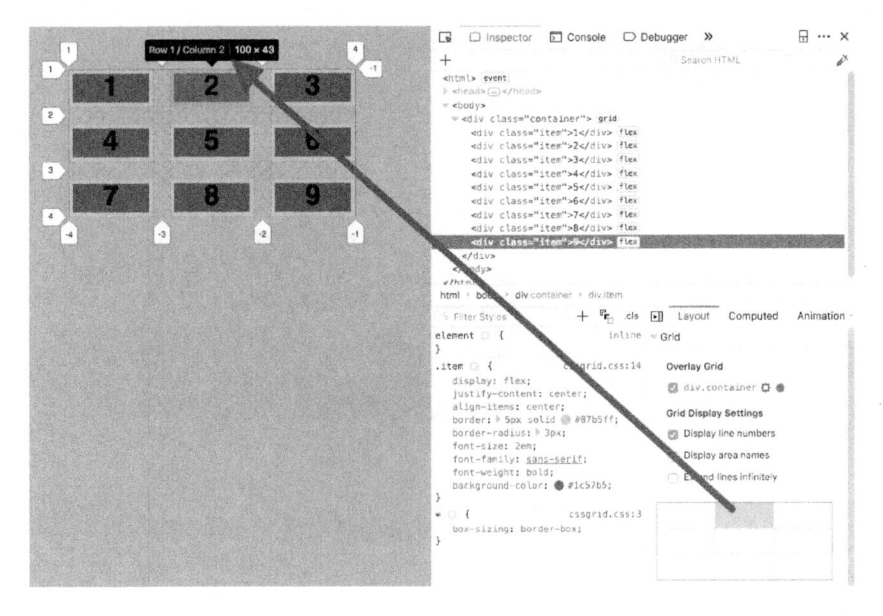

So far we've been looking at the "Grid" tab, but the "Box Model" tab also has useful information. The Box Model tab will show detailed information about any element you select, as in the image below:

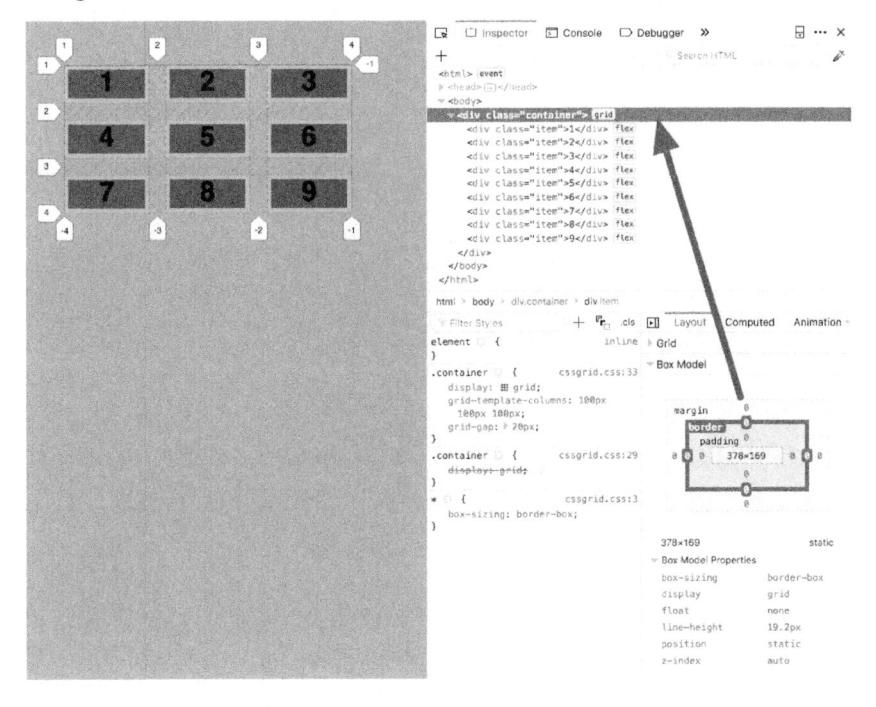

16 JORGE MONTOYA AND STEVE BURGE

These features might seem superficial with a fixed 3×3 grid, but they are very useful with bigger and more complicated grid designs.

THE GRID LINES IN FIREFOX DEV TOOLS

Let's take a closer look at the lines that are crossing and surrounding the grid.

You'll notice that these lines have different styles. If you learn to read these lines, they will help you to understand how elements are placed inside the grid.

I've used the color picker to change the lines to pink. This should make the lines easier to see in the images below.

The continuous lines show you where the grid starts and ends. Notice that there is a continuous line at both sides and on top of the grid. But there's no continuous line closing the grid container at the bottom. This is because we have not explicitly defined the grid as having three rows. The browser is implicitly organizing our nine items into three rows. We'll talk more about explicit and implicit layouts in the next chapter.

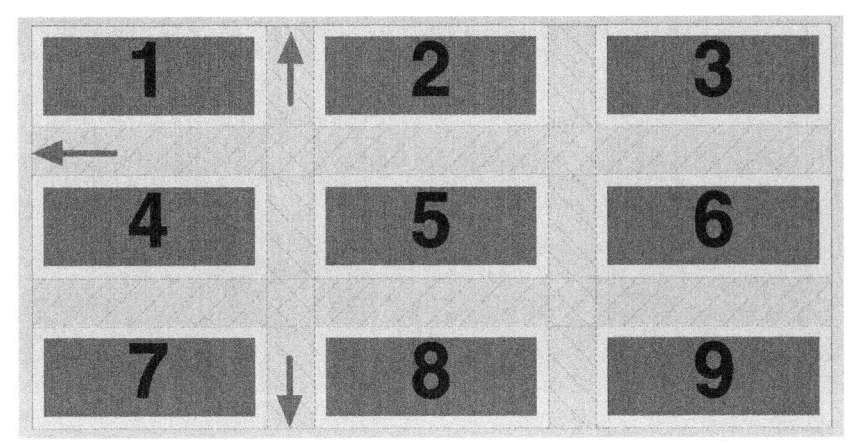

The diagonal dashed lines show you the horizontal and vertical gap between grid items.

Finally, Firefox will show you the difference between Implicit Grids and Explicit Grids.

The lines with short dots show you which grid tracks are being defined in an implicit way by the browser. You can see those dotted lines for the rows in the image below.

The lines with long-dashes show you which tracks have been explicitly defined by the CSS. You can see those dashed lines for the columns in the image below.

CHAPTER 4.

HOW TO CREATE EXPLICIT AND IMPLICIT GRIDS

In this chapter, we'll explain the difference between Implicit Grids and Explicit Grids. We've briefly touched on this feature of CSS Grid in earlier chapters, and now it's time for a more detailed explanation. Understanding the difference is the key to successfully placing rows and columns with CSS Grid.

WHAT ARE EXPLICIT AND IMPLICIT GRIDS?

To understand explicit and implicit grids, it's useful to quickly recap the code we've written so far. The main HTML code we've been using for these tutorials is shown below. This code places nine items inside a container:

```
<div class="container">
<div class="item">1</div>
<div class="item">2</div>
<div class="item">3</div>
<div class="item">4</div>
<div class="item">5</div>
<div class="item">6</div>
<div class="item">7</div>
<div class="item">8</div>
<div class="item">9</div>
</div>
```

The CSS code creates a grid container and three columns inside that container. The distance between rows and columns is 20px.

```
.container {
display: grid;
grid-template-columns: 100px 100px 100px;
grid-gap: 20px;
}
```

Notice that we do not talk about rows in this code. The browser automatically places the fourth item on the second row. The second and third rows are *implicit tracks*. Remember back to the last chapter and our work with Firefox. The rows are shown using lines with small dots to indicate that they are implicit. The columns are shown using lines with long dashes to indicate that we explicitly defined them in our CSS.

Let's change how our grid is created. Let's define the rows in the grid with the grid-template-rows property.

- Open up your css-grid.css file.
- Add the `grid-template-rows` line you see below:

```
.container {
display: grid;
grid-template-columns: 100px 100px 100px;
```

```
  grid-template-rows: 60px 60px 60px;
  grid-gap: 20px;
}
```

The explicit grid now has three columns and three rows. You can tell this by using the Firefox Grid Inspector. You can notice that there is now a continuous line "closing" the grid at the bottom, after the third row. You'll also notice that the rows use the long dashed lines as the columns. Both these changes happened because the number of rows is explicitly defined.

ADDING EXTRA ROWS TO THE GRID

Let's see what happens if we add more items to our grid.

- Open your css-grid.html file.
- Add two more items inside the grid container:

```
<div class="container">
<div class="item">1</div>
<div class="item">2</div>
<div class="item">3</div>
```

```
<div class="item">4</div>
<div class="item">5</div>
<div class="item">6</div>
<div class="item">7</div>
<div class="item">8</div>
<div class="item">9</div>
<div class="item">10</div>
<div class="item">11</div>
</div>
```

- Save the file.
- Refresh your browser and check the Grid Inspector again.

What do you notice about your new Grid? Yes, there is still a line marking the end of the explicit grid after the third row. However, the new elements were positioned by the browser in an implicit track, because there are more items than grid cells.

You do not have to declare each track and place each item manually on the grid. Web browsers are capable of placing these extra items in a logical and ordered way.

Did you notice Items 10 and 11 are slightly squashed? This is because the height of the extra row is determined by the content inside the item. To let the browser generate rows with a particular height, you can use the `grid-auto-rows` property.

- Edit your css-grid.css file.
- Add this `grid-auto-rows` property:

```
.container {
display: grid;
grid-template-columns: 100px 100px 100px;
grid-template-rows: 60px 60px 60px;
grid-auto-rows: 60px;
grid-gap: 20px;
}
```

Refresh your grid and Items 10 and 11 should now be the same size as all the other items. Because we've taken this approach, every new generated row will have a default (minimum height) of 60px.

CHAPTER 5.

HOW TO USE THE AUTOFLOW PROPERTY IN CSS GRID

In the last chapter, you saw how CSS Grid responds if you haven't defined enough rows to contain all your grid items.

In our example, grid items were automatically placed in the grid in an explicit way through the grid algorithm.

In this chapter, we'll look at the `Autoflow` property of CSS Grid. This will help us get more control over how our items are placed in the grid.

CREATE THE HTML AND CSS CODE

If you want to download the code for this chapter, you'll find it at https://github.com/OSTraining/cssgrid/tree/master/autoflow.

- Create a folder called /autoflow/.
- Create an HTML file called autoflow.html.
- Enter this code:

```
<html>

<head>
<link       rel="stylesheet"       type="text/css"
```

```
href="autoflow.css">
</head>

<div class="container">
<div class="item">1</div>
<div class="item">2</div>
<div class="item">3</div>
<div class="item">4</div>
<div class="item">5</div>
<div class="item">6</div>
</div>

</html>
```

- Create a CSS file called autoflow.css in the same folder.
- Add the following CSS.

```
/* GLOBAL STYLES */
* {
box-sizing: border-box;
}

body {
background-color: #AAA;
margin: 50px;
}

/* Each item in the grid contains numbers */
.item {

/* Center the contents of the grid items. Make
each grid item a Flex Container */
display: flex;

/* Horizontal and Vertical centering */
justify-content: center;
align-items: center;
```

```
border: 5px solid #87b5ff;
border-radius: 3px;
font-size: 2em;
font-family: sans-serif;
font-weight: bold;
background-color: #1c57b5;
}
```

- Open your autoflow.html file in a browser. It should look like the image below:

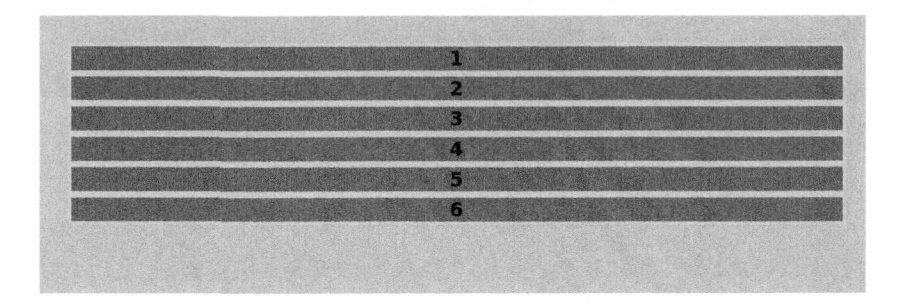

THE GRID STYLES

To declare the .container element as a grid container, add the following code to your CSS file:

```
.container {
display: grid;
width: 900px;
grid-gap: 15px;
grid-template-columns: 200px 200px 200px 200px;
grid-template-rows: 75px 75px;
}
```

The container will have a width of 900px. Each column will have a width of 200px. Each declared row will have a height of 75px.

There will be a gap between columns and rows of 15px. The grid now looks like this:

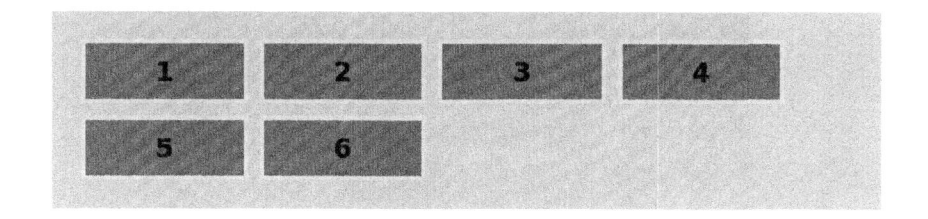

- In Firefox, turn on the Grid Inspector and enable the grid container lines.

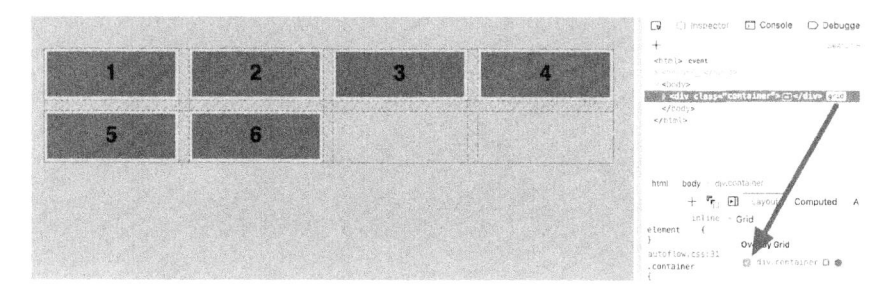

You can see that the grid container is surrounded by a solid line. All these items are placed inside the explicit grid.

- Open your autoflow.html file.
- Add three more items to the HTML structure:

```
<div class="container">
<div class="item">1</div>
<div class="item">2</div>
<div class="item">3</div>
<div class="item">4</div>
<div class="item">5</div>
<div class="item">6</div>
<div class="item">7</div>
<div class="item">8</div>
<div class="item">9</div>
</div>
```

Refresh your browser, and this is how your new grid will appear:

CSS GRID EXPLAINED 27

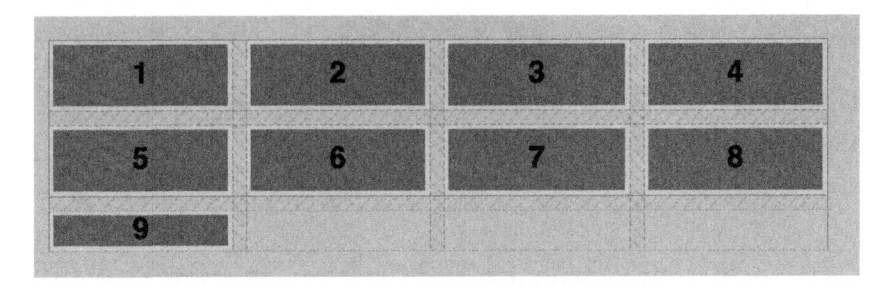

Items 1 to 8 are inside the explicit grid. Item 9 has been placed into the implicit grid. You can tell the difference by looking at the dotted line surrounded Item 9.

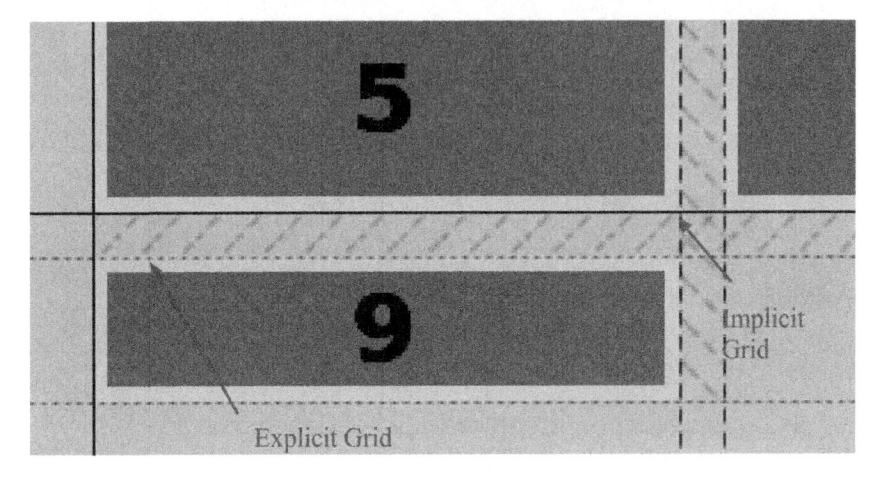

In this situation, the browser placed Item 9 in the grid with the help of a placement algorithm.

The flow of this grid is *row-based* because elements flow (wrap over) to the next row when there's no more space available. The default approach in CSS Grid is for items to flow from left to right and wrap over to the next row:

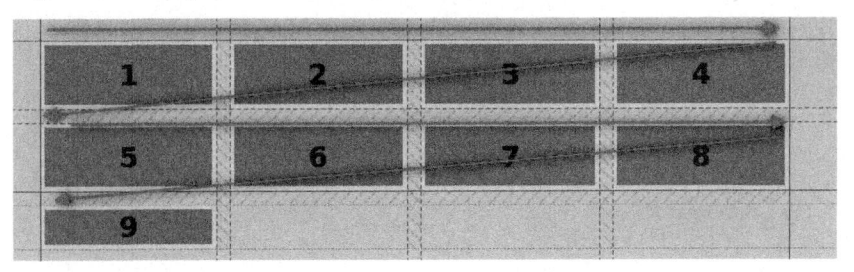

THE GRID-AUTO-FLOW PROPERTY

You don't have to keep the default left-to-right, row-based approach in CSS Grid.

The `grid-auto-flow` property allows you to place the grid items in a *column-based* flow.

- Add this `grid-auto-flow` line to your CSS file:

```
.container
{
display: grid;
width: 900px;
grid-gap: 15px;
grid-template-columns: 200px 200px 200px 200px;
grid-template-rows: 75px 75px;
grid-auto-flow: column;
}
```

The flow of the grid is now *column-based.* Item 9 is still in the explicit grid, but it has wrapped over to the next column instead of wrapping to the next row.

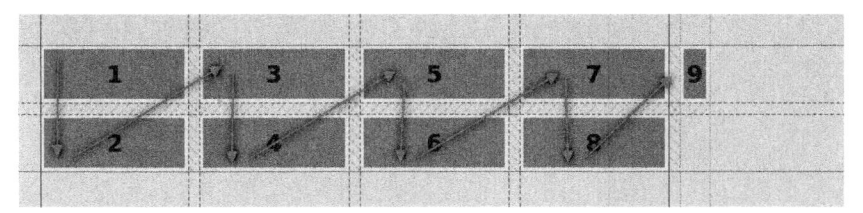

Notice the width of Item 9. We haven't declared a width for this extra column, so the browser has automatically set the width based on the content.

Let's fix the width of the extra column by updating the CSS.

- Add this `grid-auto-columns` line to your CSS:

```
.container
```

```
display: grid;
width: 900px;
grid-gap: 15px;
grid-template-columns: 200px 200px 200px 200px;
grid-template-rows: 75px 75px;
grid-auto-flow: column;
grid-auto-columns: 200px;
}
```

Each new column will have now have a width of 200px:

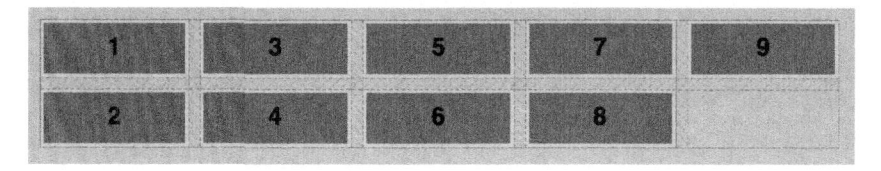

HORIZONTAL SCROLLING

Before we close this chapter, I'll note one important thing about using column-based layouts.

As you already noticed, we are using fixed units (px) in this grid. That means that if you keep adding grid items to the container, you'll get a horizontal scrolling effect in your screen.

- Add five more items to your autoflow.css file:

```
<div class="container">
<div class="item">1</div>
<div class="item">2</div>
<div class="item">3</div>
<div class="item">4</div>
<div class="item">5</div>
<div class="item">6</div>
<div class="item">7</div>
<div class="item">8</div>
<div class="item">9</div>
```

```
<div class="item">10</div>
<div class="item">11</div>
<div class="item">12</div>
<div class="item">13</div>
<div class="item">14</div>
</div>
```

Here's how your updated grid will appear:

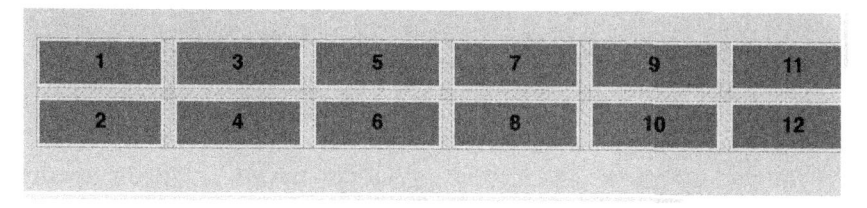

This scrolling effect will be a problem for many layouts. Fortunately, there are other ways to declare column width with relative values, such as using the `fr` unit. We'll cover those in the next chapter!

CHAPTER 6.

HOW TO USE THE FR UNIT FOR LAYOUTS

In the last chapter, we created a column-based layout using the autoflow property of CSS Grid.

However, we also saw some problems with column-based layouts. These problems were caused by using pixels, which are fixed units.

However, there are other methods to control the size of the tracks in CSS Grid. This chapter will explain those different measuring units.

CREATING THE HTML AND CSS

If you want to download the code for this chapter, you'll find it at https://github.com/OSTraining/cssgrid/tree/master/fr-unit.

- Create a folder called /fr-unit/.
- Create an HTML file called fr-unit.html inside the folder.
- Enter this code:

```
<html>

<head>
<link rel="stylesheet" type="text/css" href="fr-
```

```
unit.css">
</head>

<body>

<div class="container">
<div class="item">1</div>
<div class="item">2</div>
<div class="item">3</div>
<div class="item">4</div>
</div>

</body>

</html>
```

- Create a CSS file called fr-unit.css.
- Add the following global styles:

```
/* GLOBAL STYLES */
* {
box-sizing: border-box;
}

body {
background-color: #AAA;
margin: 50px;
}

/* Each item in the grid contains numbers */
.item {

/* Center the contents of the grid items. Make
each grid item a Flex Container */
display: flex;

/* Horizontal and Vertical centering */
justify-content: center;
```

```
align-items: center;
border: 5px solid #87b5ff;
border-radius: 3px;
font-size: 2em;
font-family: sans-serif;
font-weight: bold;
background-color: #1c57b5;
}
```

- Open the HTML file in the browser, and it should look like this:

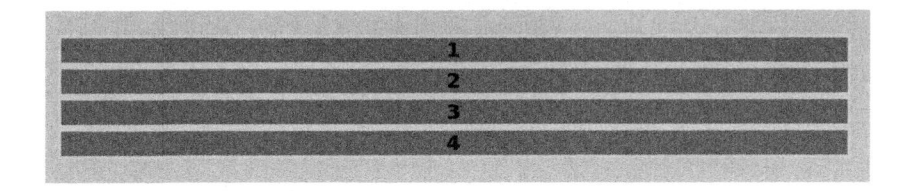

THE GRID STYLES

Let's start by using the same technique we've used throughout the book so far. We are going to declare the element with the class `container` as a grid container. We will assign a fixed column width of 200px for each item:

```
/* CSS Grid Styles */
.container {
display: grid;
grid-template-columns: 200px 200px 200px 200px;
}
```

- Refresh your browser, and your grid looks like this now:

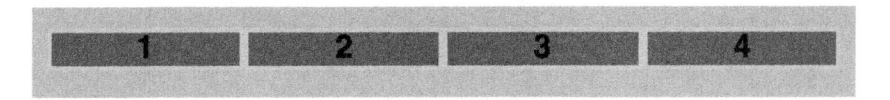

Now let's move our grid towards a more flexible approach. Let's change the fixed width units for percentages.

- Change the .container code in your CSS file:

```
.container {
display: grid;
grid-template-columns: 25% 25% 25% 25%;
}
```

- In Firefox, enable the Grid Inspector.
- Your grid will now look like the image below:

Each item is taking 25% of the available container space. The HTML container (block element) has the same width as the parent container – in this example, that is the body element.

Next, let's add some gap to the rows and columns inside the grid with the grid-gap property.

- Change the .container code in your CSS file:

```
.container {
display: grid;
grid-template-columns: 25% 25% 25% 25%;
grid-gap: 30px;
}
```

The grid container still has the same width, but the grid and the grid items have surpassed these boundaries. There is an unwanted horizontal scroll as a side effect. The reason is that the gap exists only in CSS. It's not part of the DOM or the document flow – it's pure styling.

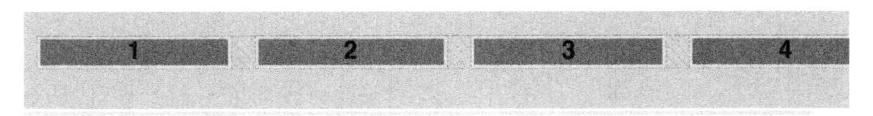

INTRODUCING THE FR UNIT

As you already have seen, both pixels and percentages can cause problems for sizing grid columns.However, CSS Grid has a solution for this issue, and that is the `fr` unit.

`fr` stands for fractional. This means that you can "fraction" the grid in a variety of ways. For example, you can have multiple equal columns or you can declare columns of different sizes.

Let's take a look at an example of using `fr` units.

- Edit your CSS code in the fr-unit.css file:

```
.container {
display: grid;
grid-template-columns: 1fr;
}
```

- Refresh your browser and take a look at the grid.

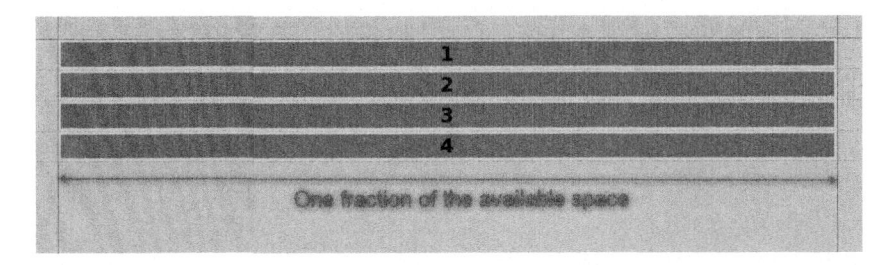

You declared one column in the CSS code, and this column is taking the available space within the container.

- Edit the CSS code once again:

```
.container {
display: grid;
grid-template-columns: 1fr 1fr 1fr 1fr;
}
```

- Refresh your browser. This is the same layout as if we've

declared percentage-based units in the CSS code:

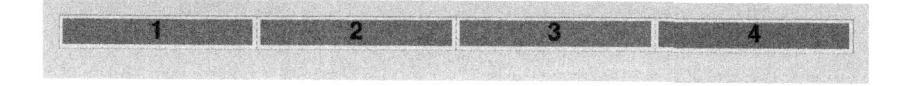

- Now add the gap between columns and rows with the `grid-gap` property:

```
container {
display: grid;
grid-template-columns: 1fr 1fr 1fr 1fr;
grid-gap: 30px;
}
```

- Refresh your browser. Each column is taking one equal fraction (of four) of the available space within the grid container.

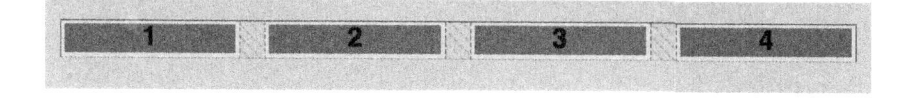

- Let's edit the CSS once again. This time, we'll create columns of different widths:

```
container {
display: grid;
grid-template-columns: 2fr 1fr;
grid-gap: 30px;
}
```

- This image below shows your grid with the new code:

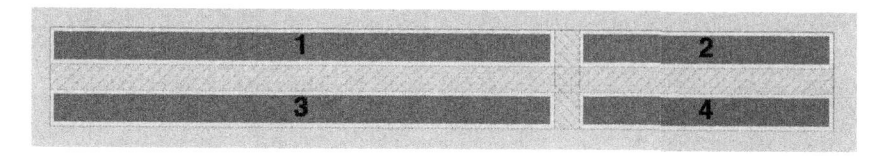

We've divided (fractioned) the grid into two columns. The first column will take two-thirds of the available space and the second column will take the other third. The grid items will explicitly place themselves.

It is possible to mix-and-match the techniques we've learned so far.

- Try this code in your fr-unit.css file:

```
.container {
display: grid;
grid-template-columns: 2fr 1fr 150px 15%;
grid-gap: 30px;
}
```

- This is how your grid will now appear:

How does CSS Grid calculate the sizes for each column? The browser works in this order:

- Column 3 must have a fixed width of 150px.
- The grid gaps must have a fixed width of 30px.
- Column 4 must be 15% of the container.
- Columns 1 and 2 do not have specific widths so they will have two thirds and one-third of the available *remaining* space each.

SIZING THE ROWS WITH FR UNIT

By default, CSS Grid items behave like block elements. This means that their height is determined by their content.

If you want to apply the `fr` unit to rows, you have to declare a fixed height for the grid container.

- Update your fr-unit.css file with this code:

```
.container {
display: grid;
height: 500px;
grid-template-columns: 2fr 1fr;
grid-template-rows: 1fr 1fr;
grid-gap: 30px;
}
```

- Refresh your browser, and this will be the end result. Your grid rows have automatically expanded to fill the 500px height.

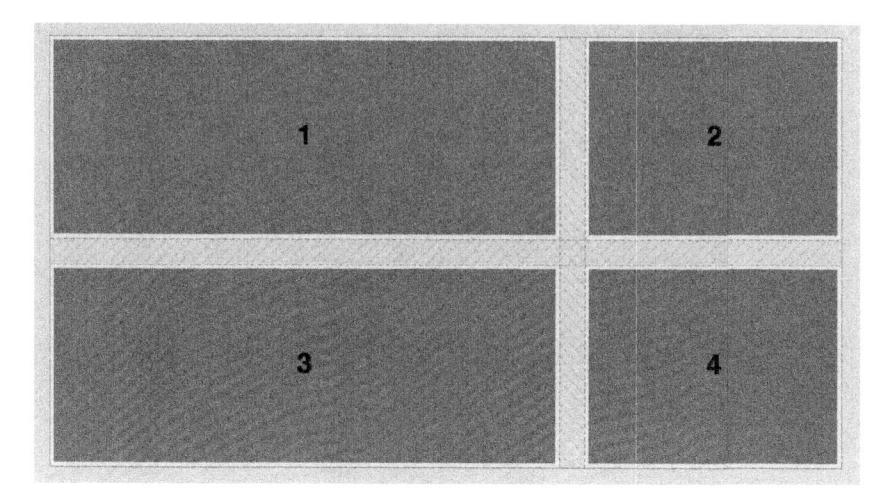

CHAPTER 7.

HOW TO SIZE TRACKS WITH THE AUTO KEYWORD

In the previous chapter, we learned about different units for sizing grid tracks.

In this chapter, I'll show you how to use the auto keyword to size tracks. We'll also discuss the repeat syntax for creating track patterns in an abbreviated way.

THE AUTO KEYWORD

In the last chapter, I mentioned that, by default, grid items behave like block elements:

- The height of grid items is determined by their content (unless the height is explicitly declared).
- The width of grid items is determined by the size you assign to the column.

The auto keyword gives you the ability to adjust the width of the grid item to the max width of its content. That means that element is responsible for sizing the column.

CREATE THE HTML AND CSS

If you want to download the code for this chapter, you'll find it here: https://github.com/OSTraining/cssgrid/tree/master/auto-keyword.

- Create a folder called /auto-keyword/.
- Create an HTML file called auto-keyword.html inside the folder.
- Enter this code:

```
<html>

<head>
<link     rel="stylesheet"     type="text/css" href="auto-keyword.css">
</head>

<body>

<div class="container">
<div class="item">1</div>
<div class="item">2</div>
<div class="item">3</div>
<div class="item">4</div>
<div class="item">5</div>
<div class="item">6</div>
<div class="item">7</div>
<div class="item">8</div>
</div>

</body>

</html>
```

- Create a CSS file called auto-keyword.css.
- Add the following styles:

```
/* GLOBAL STYLES */
* {
```

```css
box-sizing: border-box;
}

body {
background-color: #AAA;
margin: 50px;
}

/* Each item in the grid contains numbers */
.item {

/* Center the contents of the grid items. Making
each grid item a Flex Container */
display: flex;

/* Horizontal and Vertical centering */
justify-content: center;
align-items: center;
border: 5px solid #87b5ff;
border-radius: 3px;
font-size: 2em;
font-family: sans-serif;
font-weight: bold;
background-color: #1c57b5
}
```

THE CSS GRID STYLES

Our starting point will be a grid with four columns and two (implicit) rows. The gap between columns and rows will be 2rem (approx 32 px on a desktop screen):

```css
/* CSS Grid Styles */
.container {
display: grid;
grid-template-columns: 1fr 1fr 1fr 1fr;
```

```
grid-gap: 2rem;
}
```

- Open the auto-keyword.html file in your browser and this is how your grid will appear:

Let's update the CSS code and change the width of the columns. This will be our first use of the auto keyword property.

- Update your CSS code:

```
.container {
display: grid;
grid-template-columns: auto 1fr 1fr auto;
grid-gap: 2rem;
}
```

Refresh your browser. You'll notice that the items in the first and fourth columns have been resized to the width of their content.

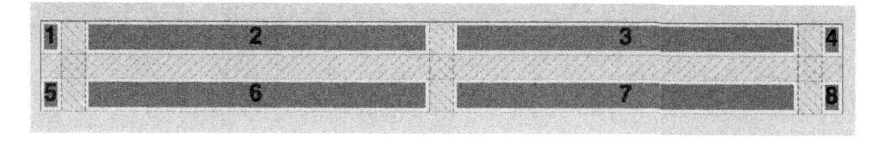

Next, let's edit the HTML markup to see if the auto keyword property really does resize the columns to fit the content.

- Update the auto-keyword.html file with these changes to Item 1:

```
<div class="container">
<div class="item">First item</div>
<div class="item">2</div>
<div class="item">3</div>
```

```
<div class="item">4</div>
<div class="item">5</div>
<div class="item">6</div>
<div class="item">7</div>
<div class="item">8</div>
</div>
```

You can see that the width of the the first column is now set to match Item 1. The second and third columns are using fr units, so they automatically adjust to fill the remaining space inside the grid container.

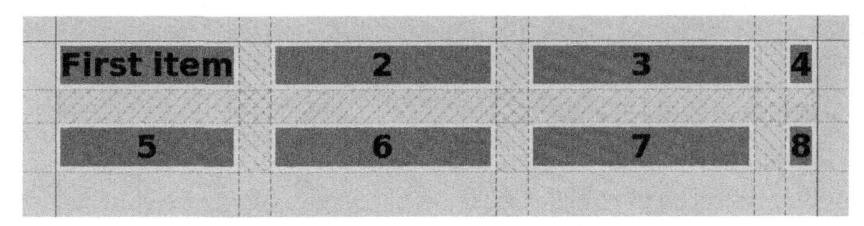

At the end of the last chapter, we saw that it's possible to mix our measuring units. Here's an example of mixed measuring units in the grid-template-columns property:

```
.container {
display: grid;
grid-template-columns: auto 1fr 2fr 10%;
grid-gap: 2rem;
}
```

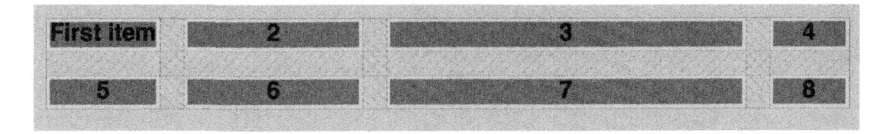

Here's how CSS grid calculates the width of these columns:

- The first column is using the auto keyword property, so it grows to match the largest item in that column.
- The fourth column will take 10% of the container width.

- The second and third columns will take one and two fractions each of the available remaining space.

THE REPEAT() NOTATION

The key to working with CSS Grid is assigning values for columns and rows. You do this using the `grid-template-columns` and `grid-template-rows` properties.

Here's an example of the type of CSS Grid we've seen so far:

```
.container {
display: grid;
grid-template-columns: 1fr 2fr 1fr 2fr;
grid-gap: 2rem;
}
```

Here's how that grid will appear in your browser:

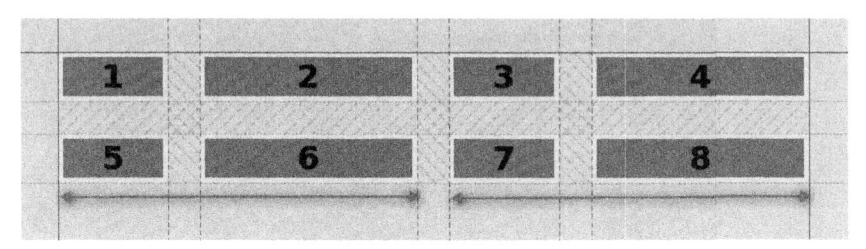

There is a pattern to this code. This pattern appears two times. We can declare this pattern with the repeat()notation. Check this CSS Grid code:

```
.container {
display: grid;
grid-template-columns: repeat(2, 1fr 2fr);
grid-gap: 2rem;
}
```

You won't see any difference in the layout in the browser. This is because we've simply declared the same thing in another way, thanks to the repeat() function.

```
grid-template-columns: repeat(2, 1fr 2fr);
```

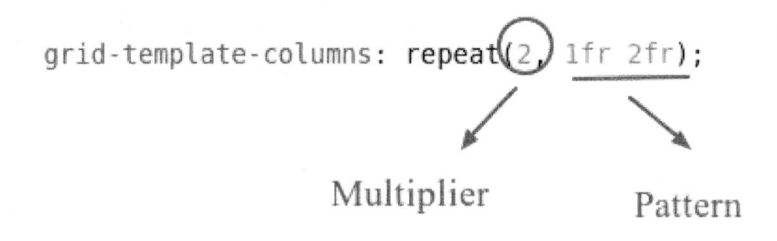

           Multiplier   Pattern

Now that you know how it works, you can create more complex patterns, for example:

```
.container {
display: grid;
grid-template-columns: repeat(2, 1fr 50px 1fr 15%);
grid-gap: 2rem;
}
```

| 1 | 2 | 3 | 4 | 5 | 6 | 7 | 8 |

CONCLUSION

The auto keyword allows you to adjust the width of a grid item according to the width of its content. The repeat syntax lets you build a predefined column (or row) pattern in an abbreviated and quicker way.

CHAPTER 8.

HOW TO SIZE GRID ITEMS WITH THE SPAN KEYWORD

So far in this book, we've seen that grid items flow one after another. Your grid items will automatically place themselves into the grid, taking a grid cell each.

We have been sizing the grid container and testing the different ways to generate tracks. However, we have not dealt with the items themselves.

In this chapter, we'll focus on the grid items. You'll learn how to determine the width of an item inside the grid container with the span keyword. You are going to span the items to a specific width or height across multiple tracks.

CREATE THE HTML AND CSS

The code for this chapter is available at https://github.com/OSTraining/cssgrid/tree/master/span-keyword.

- Create a folder called /span-keyword/.
- Create an HTML file called span-keyword.html inside the folder.
- Enter this code:

```
<html>

<head>
<link      rel="stylesheet"      type="text/css"
href="span-keyword.css">
</head>

<body>

<div class="container">
<div class="item item1">1</div>
<div class="item item2">2</div>
<div class="item item3">3</div>
<div class="item item4">4</div>
<div class="item item5">5</div>
<div class="item item6">6</div>
<div class="item item7">7</div>
<div class="item item8">8</div>
<div class="item item9">9</div>
<div class="item item10">10</div>
<div class="item item11">11</div>
<div class="item item12">12</div>
<div class="item item13">13</div>
</div>

</body>

</html>
```

Next, let's create the CSS that you will apply to the items you just created.

- Create a CSS file called span-keyword.css.
- Add the following global styles:

```
/* GLOBAL STYLES */
* {
```

```css
box-sizing: border-box;
}

body {
background-color: #AAA;
margin: 50px;
}

/* Each item in the grid contains numbers */

.item {
/* Center the contents of the grid items. Making each grid item a Flex Container */

display: flex;

/* Horizontal and Vertical centering */

justify-content: center;
align-items: center;
border: 5px solid #87b5ff;
border-radius: 3px;
font-size: 2em;
font-family: sans-serif;
font-weight: bold;
background-color: #1c57b5
}
```

Here is how your page will look with this HTML and CSS code:

CREATE THE CSS GRID

Now let's create the grid. Your starting point will be a grid with four columns and four (implicit) rows. The gap between columns and rows will be 2rem, which is approximately 32 px on a desktop screen:

```
/* CSS Grid Styles */

.container {
display: grid;
grid-template-columns: repeat(4, 1fr);
grid-gap: 2rem;
}
```

Once the grid is ready, you'll see that Item 13 automatically creates a fourth row:

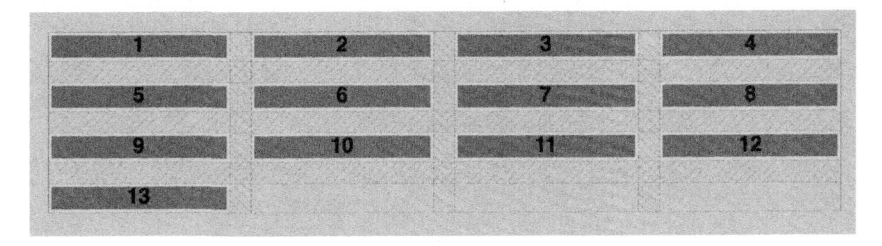

RESIZING THE ITEMS

Now let's get to the heart of this chapter. We are going to resize individual grid items. We are going to double the size of the third item in the grid:

- Add this CSS code to your span-keyword.css file. This code is targeting the .item3 class:

```
.item3 {
grid-column: span 2;
}
```

- Refresh your browser, and this image shows what you'll see:

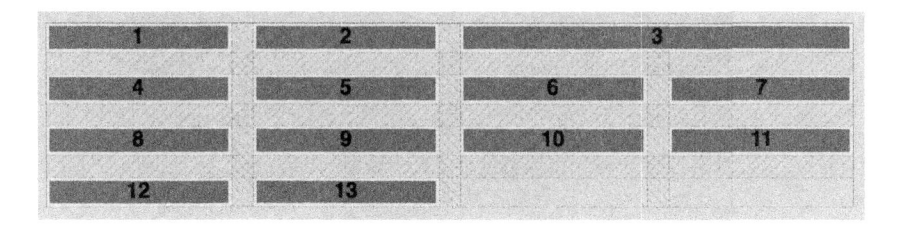

You'll see that Item 3 now spans across two column tracks. All the items from Item 4 onward have skipped one spot to the next available cell. The browser takes care of this automatically.

Let's see what happens if we make that item even wider:

- Edit the code and let's stretch Item 3 so that it spans across three columns.

```
.item3 {
grid-column: span 3;
}
```

- Item 3 is now wider than the available space on the first row of the grid, so it wraps over to the next row.

Now let's get really funky with the item size. We are going to make Item 3 stretch across multiple rows and columns.

- Edit the CSS code once again to span Item 3 across rows:

```
.item3 {
grid-column: span 3;
grid-row: span 3;
}
```

- Refresh your browser, and you can see that Item 3 now spans across three columns and three rows. Items 4, 5, and 6 took the available cells on the right side. Item 7 starts a new row.

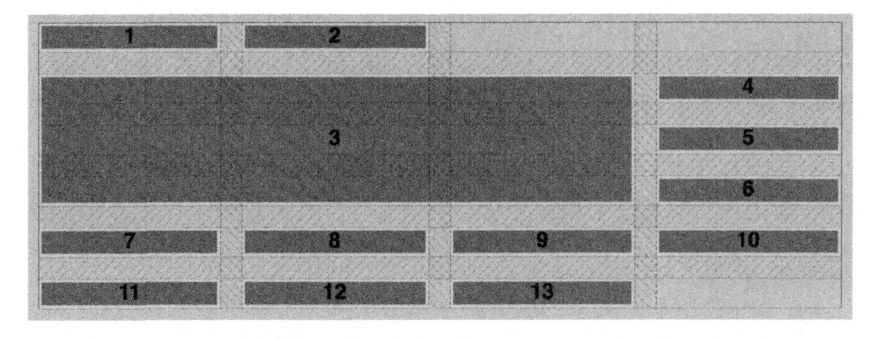

If you're wondering about the blank space on the upper right, there are ways in CSS Grid to place items on any cell or area of the grid. I'll show you how to do that in a future chapter.

A NOTE OF CAUTION

There are limits to how creative you can be with CSS Grid. Let's do something that I would not recommend doing in a production environment.

- Edit the CSS code one more time:

```
.item3 {
grid-column: span 5;
grid-row: span 2;
}
```

Item 3 now covers five columns. It overlaps the whole implicit grid and takes one more track from the explicit grid. The width of this extra track is determined by the widest content inside that column. In this example, the widest content in that column is Item 13. The vertical span has also disappeared and so the grid is broken.

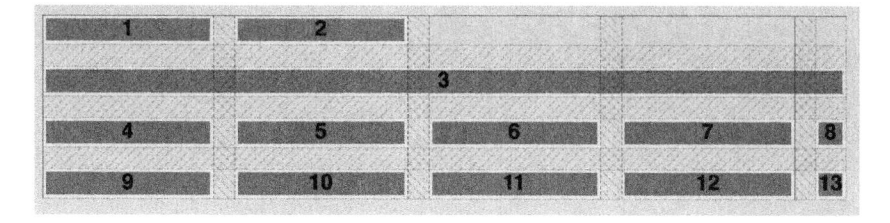

CHAPTER 9.

HOW TO USE LINE NUMBERS IN CSS GRID

In the last chapter, you learned about the `span` keyword in CSS Grid. We used this feature to increase or decrease the size of grid items.

But, what if you want to have more visual control about what's happening on the grid?

It is possible to place grid items with the help of the numbered lines that compose the grid. This chapter will explain this feature.

CREATE THE HTML AND CSS

You can download the code for this chapter on Github: https://github.com/OSTraining/cssgrid/tree/master/line-numbers.

- Create a folder called /line-numbers/.
- Create an HTML file called line-numbers.html inside the folder.
- Enter this code:

```
<html>

<head>
<link       rel="stylesheet"       type="text/css"
```

```
    href="line-numbers.css">
</head>

<body>

<div class="container">
<div class="item item1">1</div>
<div class="item item2">2</div>
<div class="item item3">3</div>
<div class="item item4">4</div>
</div>

</body>

</html>
```

- Create a CSS file called line-numbers.css.
- Add the following styles:

```
/* GLOBAL STYLES */
* {
box-sizing: border-box;
}

body {
background-color: #AAA;
margin: 50px;
}

/* Each item in the grid contains numbers */
.item {

/* Center the contents of the grid items. Making
each grid item a Flex Container */
display: flex;

/* Horizontal and Vertical centering */
justify-content: center;
```

```
align-items: center;
border: 5px solid #87b5ff;
border-radius: 3px;
font-size: 2em;
font-family: sans-serif;
font-weight: bold;
background-color: #1c57b5
}
```

- With this code in place, this is how your grid will appear:

LINE NUMBERS IN CSS GRID

Our new grid will be extremely basic at first. It will only have four defined columns. The gap between columns and rows will be 2rem, which is approximately 32px.

- Add this to your line-numbers.css file:

```
/* CSS Grid Styles */

.container {
display: grid;
grid-template-columns: repeat(4, 1fr);
grid-gap: 2rem;
}
```

- Turn on the Grid Inspector in Firefox.
- Choose to "Display line numbers" and to "Extend lines infinitely".

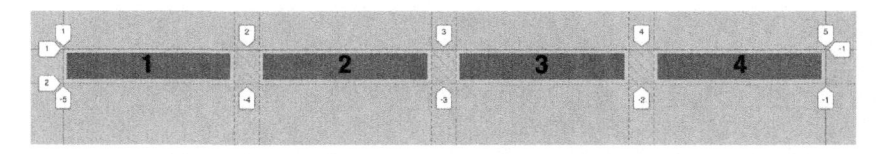

As you can see, the items in the grid are separated by numbered lines.

- Item 1 starts at line #1 and ends at line #2.
- Item 2 starts at line #2 and ends at line #3.

When you're thinking about this grid, don't consider the gap. Remember that the gaps are pure styling.

To understand this a little bit better, let's take a look at an example with the `span` keyword that you saw in an earlier chapter.

- Add this to your CSS file:

```
.item3 {
grid-column: span 2;
}
```

- When you refresh your browser, you'll see that Item 3 now spans two columns from line #3 to line #5.

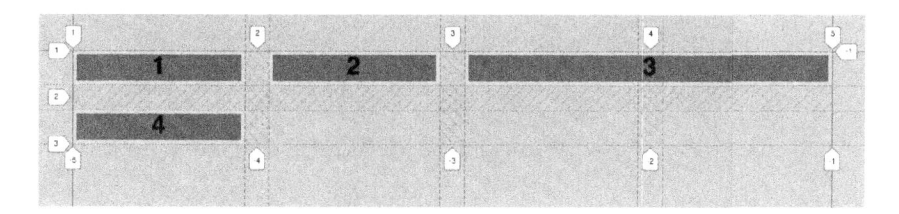

The `grid-column` property we used in this CSS is a shorthand for `grid-column-start` and `grid-column-end`. The extended code that produces the same results, in this case, would be:

```
.item3 {
grid-column-start: span 2;
grid-column-end: auto;
}
```

This code is telling the browser where to place Item 3. The instructions are to start Item 3 from where it's located and to span it over two vertical tracks.

The line numbers are used to mark the starting and ending position of items within the grid. This visual aid helps you save time and organize your code better, especially with complex layouts.

The slightly longer code you see above is going to be very helpful throughout this chapter. We can use that code to get even more specific about where Item 3 should be placed.

Try this code in your line-spacing.css file:

```
.item3 {
grid-column-start: 2;
grid-column-end: 5;
}
```

Item 3 starts at line #2 and ends at line #5 spanning over three vertical tracks. This is how your grid now appears:

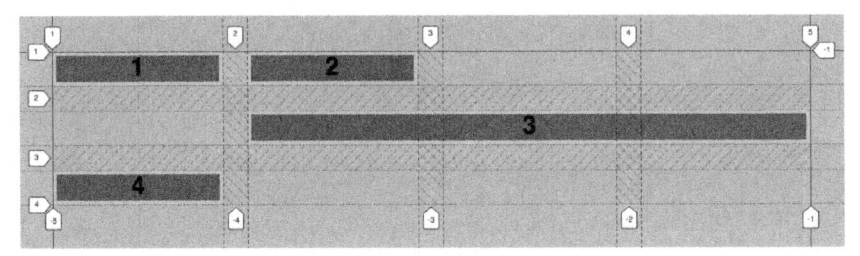

The shorthand property for that code is as follows:

```
.item3 {
grid-column: 2 / 5;
}
```

Let's use that shorthand version of the code to rearrange our grid again.

- Edit the CSS code:

```
.item1 {
grid-column: 3 / 4;
}

.item3 {
grid-column: 2 / 5;
}
```

The image below shows the impact of this code on your grid:

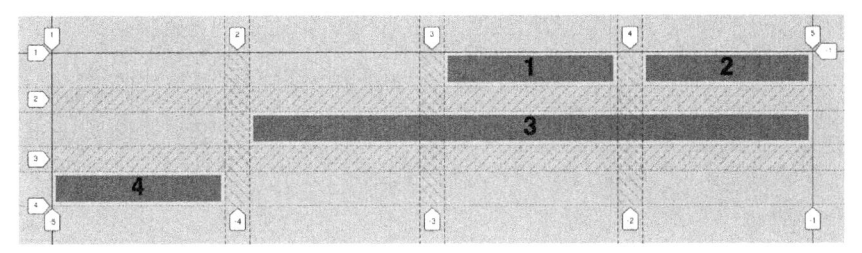

You have seen several examples of how we can use the line numbers in CSS grid. But, what about those negative numbers pointing to the grid lines?

Those negative numbers help you see the grid "backwards". This means that the last line in the grid is -1, the penultimate line is -2 and so on. Let's see how that would work in our code.

- Update your CSS code:

```
.item1 {
grid-column: -4 / -2;
}
```

You'll notice that Item 1 now spans two columns instead of one. Item 1 starts at line -4 and spans two columns to the right, ending at line -2.

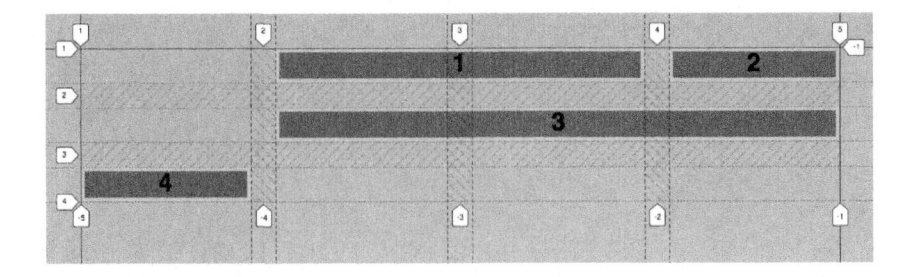

USE LINE NUMBERS TO CONTROL COLUMNS

Let's see how these line number techniques can be applied to columns as well as rows.

- Remove the .item1 and .item3 selectors from your line-numbers.css file.
- Update this part of the CSS code:

```
.container {
display: grid;
grid-template-columns: repeat(4, 1fr);
grid-template-rows: repeat(6, 1fr);
grid-gap: 2rem;
}
```

Your grid will now look like this image below. The grid has four columns (vertical lines #1 to #5) and six rows (horizontal lines #1 to #7).

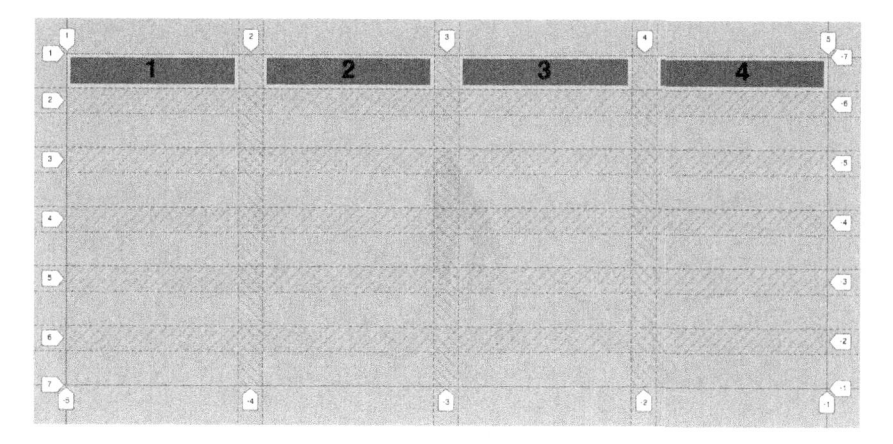

Let's write some CSS code to take advantage of that extra space. We're going to create a unique size for all four items:

```
.item1 {
grid-column: 1 / 2;
grid-row: 7 / 6;
}

.item2 {
grid-column: 2 / 3;
grid-row: 7 / 5
}

.item3 {
grid-column: 3 / 4;
grid-row: 7 / 4;
}

.item4 {
grid-column: 4 / 5;
grid-row: -1 / -5;
}
```

This image below shows the end-result of your changes:

CSS GRID EXPLAINED 61

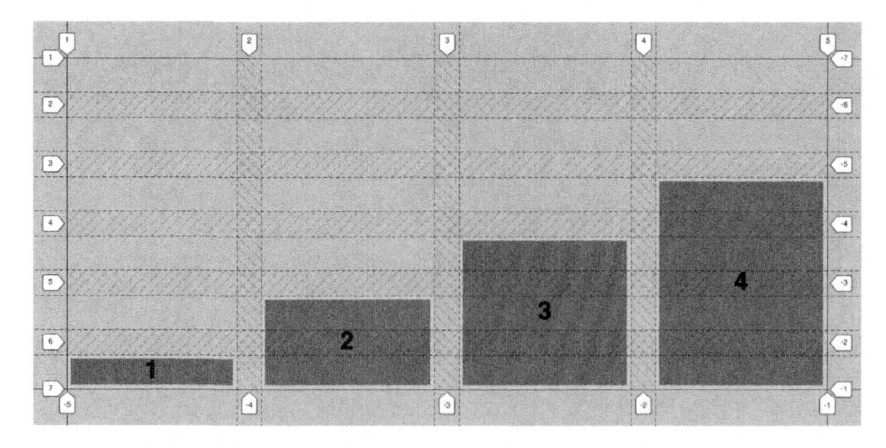

Now it's time for you to play. Try to explore all possibilities available with the line based placement.

For example, you can span Item 3 over two columns to the right and see what happens. Then do the same but spanning it two columns to the left.

After that, place the .item3 selector before .item2 in the CSS code. Does that change the layout? What happens if you change the order of the items in the markup?

CHAPTER 10.

HOW TO LAYER ITEMS IN CSS GRID

In the first chapters of this book, we saw that browsers have an auto-placement algorithm. Using this algorithm, items are automatically placed inside empty grid cells. Items will not overlap with each other when using this auto-placement.

In the last chapter, you also learned how to place grid items anywhere on the grid with the help of the grid's numbered lines.

Using grid numbers, it becomes possible to layer items. You can do this because grid numbers allow you to define the start and end positions of every item. You can also layer items in three dimensions using the CSS z-index property.

Let's look at some examples and show you how to layer items in CSS Grid.

CREATE THE HTML AND CSS

The code for this chapter is online here: https://github.com/OSTraining/cssgrid/tree/master/layers.

- Create a folder called /layers/.
- Create an HTML file called layers.html inside the folder.
- Enter this code:

```html
<html>

<head>
<link     rel="stylesheet"     type="text/css" href="layers.css">
</head>

<body>

<div class="container">
<div class="item item1">1</div>
<div class="item item2">2</div>
<div class="item item3">3</div>
<div class="item item4">4</div>
</div>

</body>

</html>
```

Next, let's create the CSS that you will apply to the items you just created.

- Create a CSS file called layers.css.
- Add the following global styles:

```css
/* GLOBAL STYLES */
* {
box-sizing: border-box;
}

body {
background-color: #AAA;
margin: 50px;
}

/* Each item in the grid contains numbers */
```

```css
.item {
/* Center the contents of the grid items. Make
each grid item a Flex Container */
display: flex;

/* Horizontal and Vertical centering */
justify-content: center;
align-items: center;
border: 5px solid black;
border-radius: 3px;
font-size: 2em;
font-family: sans-serif;
font-weight: bold;
}
```

CREATE THE CSS GRID

Our grid for this exercise will have three columns and three rows. The gap between columns and rows will be 2rem, which is approximately 32px.

Each one of the items will have a different color so we can easily identify it:

```css
/* CSS Grid Styles */
.container {
display: grid;
grid-template-columns: repeat(3, 1fr);
grid-template-rows: repeat(3, 150px);
grid-gap: 2rem;
}
```

```css
.item1 {
background-color: #f7cb2a;
}

.item2 {
background-color: #00407b;
}

.item3 {
background-color: #469c07;
}

.item4 {
background-color: #f25039;
}
```

- This image shows your new grid with this extra CSS:

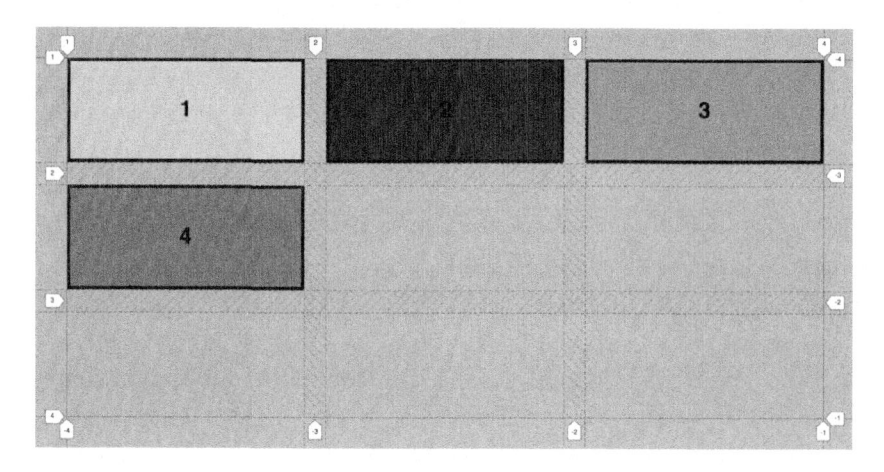

CREATE OVERLAPPING ITEMS

We can now use the line placement techniques that we learned in the previous chapter. We're going to change the position and dimensions of the grid items.

Here's the layout that we're going to implement:

- Each item will span over two rows and two columns.
- Each item will start from a different corner of the grid.

Remember that our grid has three columns and three rows. So what will happen when we try to add four items, each spanning across two rows and two columns? Let's find out!

- Update your layer.css file with this new code:

```css
.item1 {
background-color: #f7cb2a;
grid-column: 1 / 3;
grid-row: 1 / 3;
}

.item2 {
background-color: #00407b;
grid-column: 2 / 4;
grid-row: 1 / 3;
}

.item3 {
background-color: #469c07;
grid-column: 1 / 3;
grid-row: 2 / 4;
}

.item4 {
background-color: #f25039;
grid-column: 2 / 4;
grid-row: 2 / 4;
}
```

- Your grid looks now like the image below.

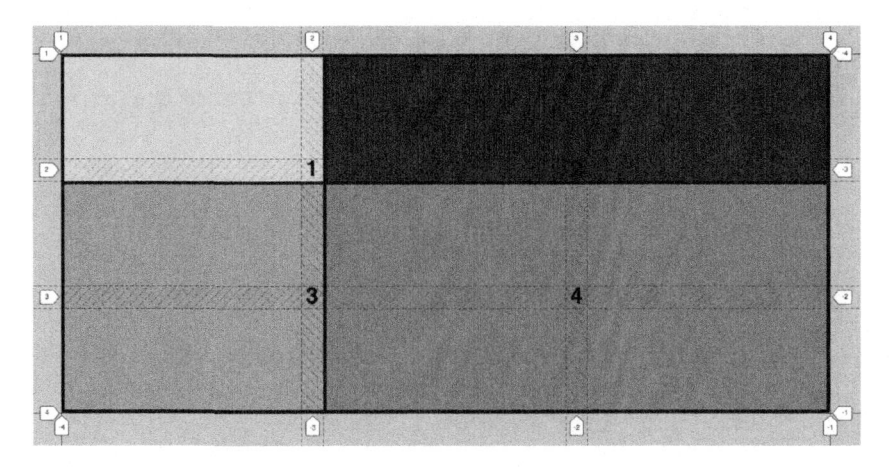

As you already have noticed, the item that comes last in the source order of the markup overlaps all other items. In this case, Item 4 is the upper layer and is hiding part of all the other items.

Let's see what happens if we reverse the ordering of the layers. We're going to make item1 into the uppermost layer. We can do this with the z-index property.

- Update the CSS code in your layers.css file:

```
.item1 {
background-color: #f7cb2a;
grid-column: 1 / 3;
grid-row: 1 / 3;
z-index: 10;
}
```

- Refresh your grid and this is what you'll see. Item 4 still overlaps Item 3 and Item 2. However, Item 1 is now layered over all of them.

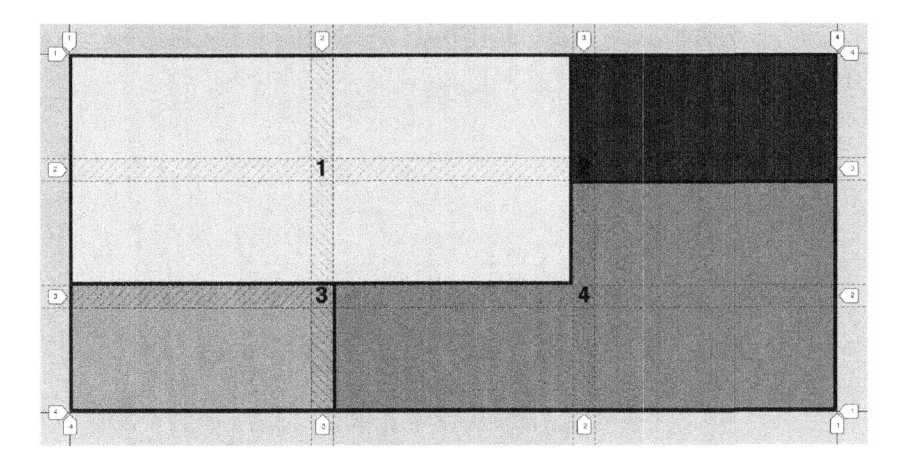

In the next step, let's place Item 3 over Item 4 but still underneath Item 1. To do this, we need to choose a lower value for the z-index property when targeting Item 3.

```
.item3 {
background-color: #469c07;
grid-column: 1 / 3;
grid-row: 2 / 4;
z-index: 8;
}
```

- Now Item 3 overlaps Item 2 and Item 4.

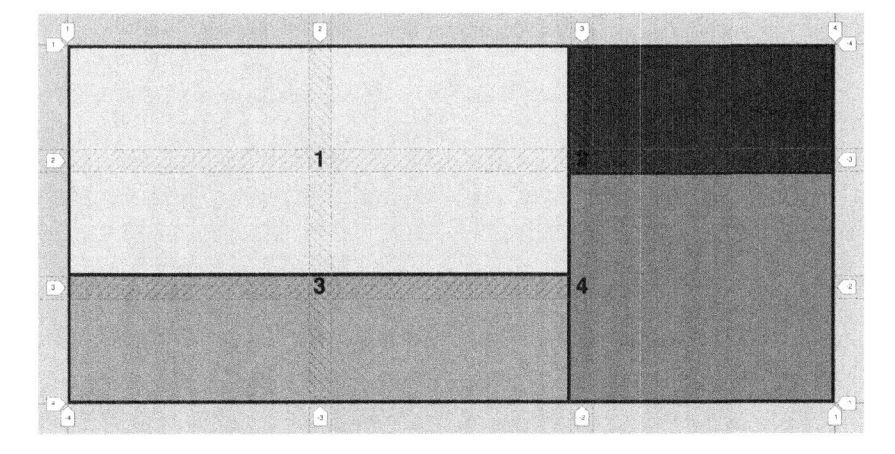

Notice that Item 4 is still overlapping Item 2. This is because Item

2 doesn't have a `z-index` and Item 4 still comes after Item 2 in the source order of the HTML code.

- Edit the CSS code once again:

```
.item2 {
background-color: #00407b;
grid-column: 2 / 4;
grid-row: 1 / 3;
z-index: 9;
}
```

- Now Item 2 is on top of Item 3 and Item 2, but still underneath Item 1. After all the changes we've made, Item 4 has gone from being the most visible item and is now the least visible item.

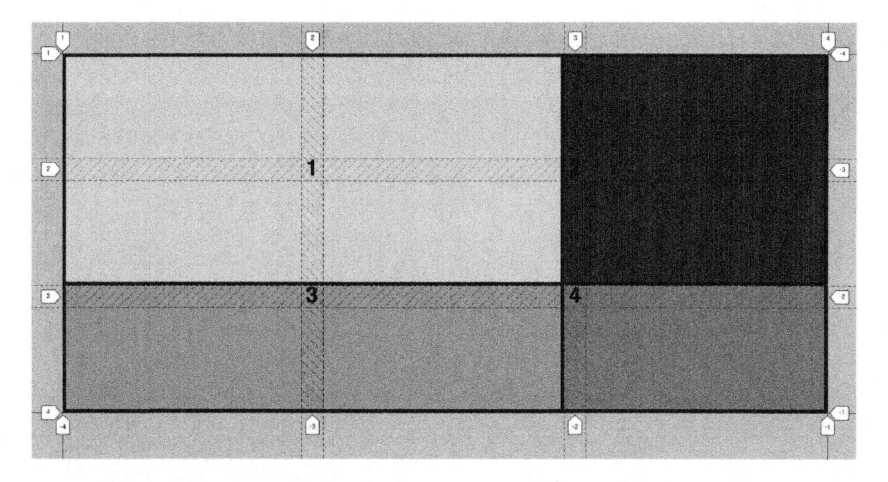

One way to check the layering is by adding transparency to Item 1:

```
.item1 {
background-color: #f7cb2a;
grid-column: 1 / 3;
grid-row: 1 / 3;
z-index: 10;
```

```
opacity: 0.35;
}
```

This transparency approach will work even for items that have been declared with the position: static property.

```
.item1 {
position: static;
background-color: #f7cb2a;
grid-column: 1 / 3;
grid-row: 1 / 3;
z-index: 10;
}
```

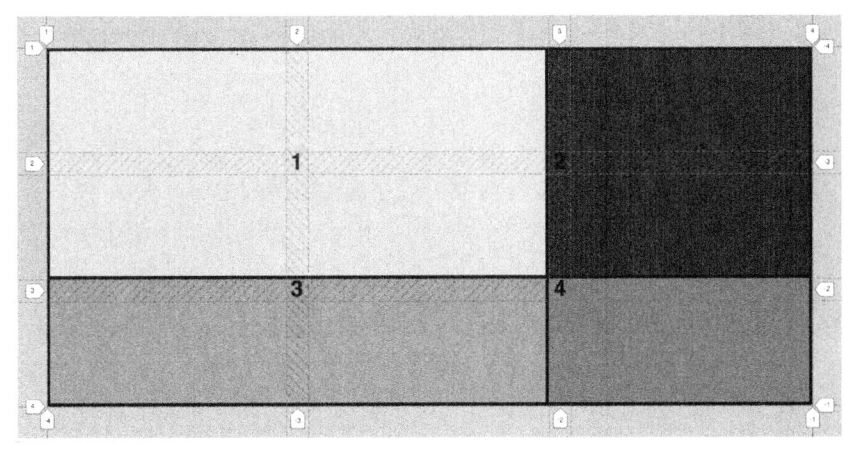

CHAPTER 11.

HOW TO USE LINE NAMES IN CSS GRID

Previously, we learned how to place items according to the numbered lines in CSS Grid.

These line numbers are very useful. You can place your items anywhere in your grid, simply by referencing the line numbers.

However, humans often find it easier to process names rather than numbers. Plus, if you have a web design background, you have much more experience with using names for website regions. CSS Grid allows you to give names to lines and refer to those words for item placement.

This chapter will explain how to name the lines that compose CSS Grid.

THE LAYOUT

We're going to build a simple layout with a header, a footer, and a content area in the center that is surrounded by two sidebars. The left sidebar will contain relevant information related to the content, and the right sidebar is for placing ads.

Header		
Articles	Content	Ads
Footer		

CREATE THE HTML AND CSS

The code for this chapter is available on Github: https://github.com/OSTraining/cssgrid/tree/master/line-names.

- Create a folder called /line-names/.
- Create an HTML file called line-names.html inside the folder.
- Enter this code:

```
<html>

<head>
<link     rel="stylesheet"     type="text/css"
href="line-names.css">
</head>

<body>
```

```html
<div class="container">
<div class="item header">Header</div>
<div class="item content">Content</div>
<div class="item sb-right">Articles</div>
<div class="item footer">Footer</div>
<div class="item ads">Ads</div>
</div>

</body>

</html>
```

Let's take a look at the structure of this markup.

As you can see, the order of the markup does not match our layout image. This is actually ideal, because we can place the relevant content on top and the less relevant content will go further down in the source order of the file.

We'll place these items in the grid using CSS.

- Create a CSS file called names.css.
- Add the following global styles:

```css
/* GLOBAL STYLES */
* {
box-sizing: border-box;
}

body {
background-color: #AAA;
margin: 0px 50px 50px;
}

/* Each item in the grid contains numbers */
.item {

/* Center the contents of the grid items. Making
```

```
each grid item a Flex Container */
display: flex;

/* Horizontal and Vertical centering */
justify-content: center;
align-items: center;
border: 5px solid #87b5ff;
border-radius: 3px;
font-size: 2em;
font-family: sans-serif;
font-weight: bold;
background-color: #1c57b5
}
```

- Here's how your grid will now appear:

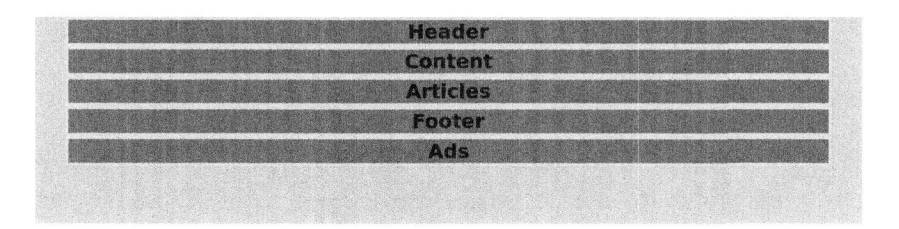

CREATE THE CSS GRID

We need a grid with three columns for the sidebars and content area and three rows for the header, main and footer containers. There will be a separation between columns of 1rem, which is about 16px in a desktop screen.

```
/*CSS Grid styles */
.container {
display: grid;
grid-template-columns: 3fr 5fr 3fr;
grid-template-rows: auto auto auto;
grid-column-gap: 1rem;
}
```

- Turn on the Firefox Grid Inspector.
- Choose to display line numbers and to extend lines infinitely:

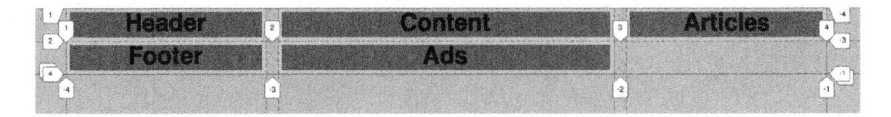

You may be wondering why our CSS splits into eleven vertical tracks instead of ten or twelve. The only reason for that is because you can. This is part of the flexibility provided by CSS Grid and its layout possibilities.

DECLARING LINE NAMES

In order to use line names, you have to declare them first. The notation for declaring a line is as follows:

```
[first-line]
```

The names of the lines are declared inside the grid-template-columns and grid-template-rows properties. A line can have two or more different names with this notation:

```
[first-line start-line]
```

This line can be referenced by either of its names.

You cannot declare a line with two particular values: 'auto' and 'span'. Please, be aware not to use these keywords when assigning names to the lines of your grid.

A vertical and a horizontal line can share the same name within a grid.

Let's take a look at the layout mockup once again:

	Header	
Articles	Content	Ads
	Footer	

The grid is composed of four lines from top to bottom and four lines from left to right. We can now define names for these lines and then declare them in the CSS file.

You can name the lines whatever you want but make sure you choose relevant names, in order to work more easily.

Each line will have two different names according to its position inside the grid:

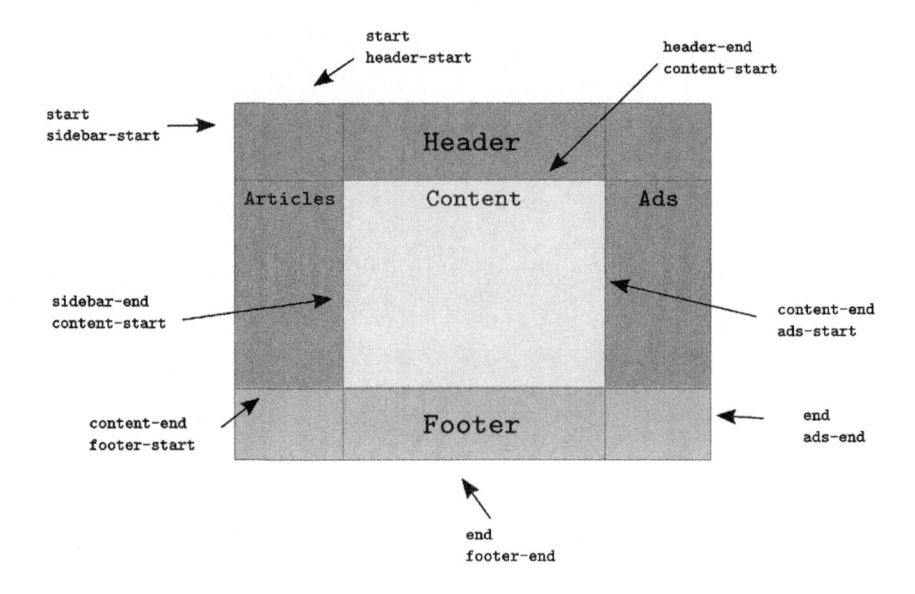

[Figure: Grid layout diagram showing Header, Articles, Content, Ads, and Footer regions with labeled grid lines: start/header-start, header-end/content-start, sidebar-start, sidebar-end/content-start, content-end/ads-start, content-end/footer-start, end/ads-end, end/footer-end]

- Update the following CSS code:

```
.container
{
display: grid;
grid-template-columns: [start sidebar-start] 3fr [sidebar-end content-start] 5fr [content-end ads-start] 3fr [end ads-end];
grid-template-rows: [start header-start] auto [header-end content-start] auto [content-end footer-start] auto [end footer-end];
grid-column-gap: 1rem;
}
```

After adding that code, you won't see any visual changes in your grid. However, we're now ready to start writing the CSS.

PLACING GRID ITEMS WITH CSS

Let's place the items in our grid, according to the layout image at the start of the chapter.

Just like placing items with line numbers, you have to position the item using the grid-column and grid-row properties. The only difference from earlier chapters is that we'll use the names of the lines (instead of their numbers).

- Update the following CSS code:

```
/*CSS Grid styles */
.container {
display: grid;
grid-template-columns: [start sidebar-start] 3fr [sidebar-end content-start] 5fr [content-end ads-start] 3fr [end ads-end];
grid-template-rows: [start header-start] auto [header-end content-start] auto [content-end footer-start] auto [end footer-end];
grid-column-gap: 1rem;
}

.header {
grid-column: start / end;
grid-row: start / header-end;
}

.articles {
grid-column: start / sidebar-end;
grid-row: header-end / footer-start;
}

.content {
grid-column: content-start / content-end;
grid-row: content-start / content-end;
}

.footer {
grid-column: start / end;
grid-row: footer-start / footer-end;
}
```

```
.ads {
grid-column: ads-start / end;
grid-row: header-end / footer-start;
}
```

- Refresh your browser, and this is what you'll see:

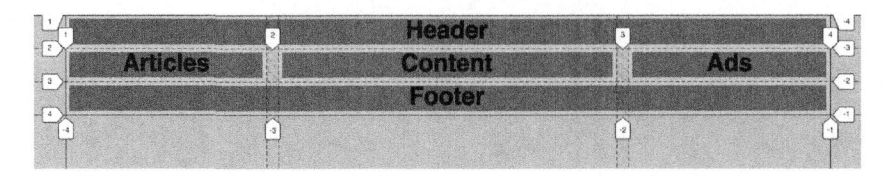

As you already know, the height of each one of the rows will be determined by its content. Our grid has the same layout as the mockup, but the height of each region is incorrect.

Let's tweak the CSS code again. We're going to set a height value for the grid container of 100vh, which is the height of the screen. We're also going to divide the row space with these values: 3fr 6fr and 2fr:

```
.container {
display: grid;
grid-template-columns: [start sidebar-start] 3fr [sidebar-end content-start] 5fr [content-end ads-start] 3fr [end ads-end];
grid-template-rows: [start header-start] 3fr [header-end content-start] 6fr [content-end footer-start] 2fr [end footer-end];
grid-column-gap: 1rem;
height: 100vh;
}
```

- Now our grid looks like a real website layout!

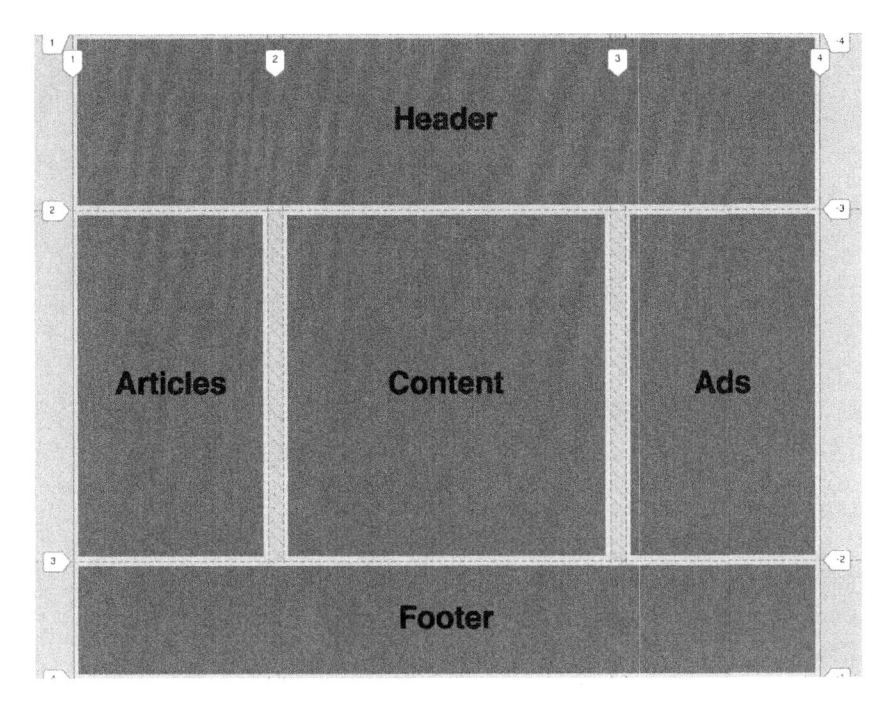

Line names are very useful when dealing with large and more complex grids because they make it easier for humans to find a location on the grid, in order to position items in it.

CHAPTER 12.

HOW TO PLACE ITEMS WITH GRID TEMPLATE AREAS

In the previous chapters, we learned how to place items on the grid using the span keyword and using line-based placement.

There's another method for placing items on the grid. You can create named areas inside the grid and then position the items on these areas.

The `grid-template-areas` property allows you to describe how the layout looks. Then with the `grid-area` property, you will be able to place those items in the areas you've defined.

THE LAYOUT

As in the last chapter, we're going to build a simple layout with a header, a content section, a footer, and two sidebars. The grid will be divided into the three columns and three rows:

```
          Header

Articles  Content   Ads



          Footer
```

CREATE THE HTML AND CSS

You can find the code for this chapter here: https://github.com/OSTraining/cssgrid/tree/master/areas.

- Create a folder called /areas/.
- Create an HTML file called areas.html inside the folder.
- Enter this code:

```
<html>

<head>
<link        rel="stylesheet"        type="text/css"
href="areas.css">
</head>

<body>

<div class="container">
<div class="item header">Header</div>
```

```html
<div class="item content">Content</div>
<div class="item articles">Articles</div>
<div class="item footer">Footer</div>
<div class="item ads">Ads</div>
</div>

</body>

</html>
```

As you already know, the source order of the markup is not relevant to the layout. The placement of the items is done with CSS.

- Create a CSS file called areas.css.
- Add the following styles:

```css
/* GLOBAL STYLES */

* {
box-sizing: border-box;
}

body {
background-color: #AAA;
margin: 0px 50px 50px;
}

/* Each item in the grid contains numbers */
.item {

/* Center the contents of the grid items. Making each grid item a Flex Container */
display: flex;

/* Horizontal and Vertical centering */
justify-content: center;
align-items: center;
```

```
border: 5px solid #87b5ff;
border-radius: 3px;
font-size: 2em;
font-family: sans-serif;
font-weight: bold;
background-color: #1c57b5
}
```

CREATE THE CSS GRID

We need a grid with three columns for the sidebars and content area and three rows for the header, main and footer containers.

```
/*CSS Grid styles */

.container {
display: grid;
grid-template-columns: 3fr 5fr 3fr;
grid-template-rows: auto auto auto;
}
```

- Turn on the Firefox Grid inspector.
- Make sure you check the "Display area names" option.

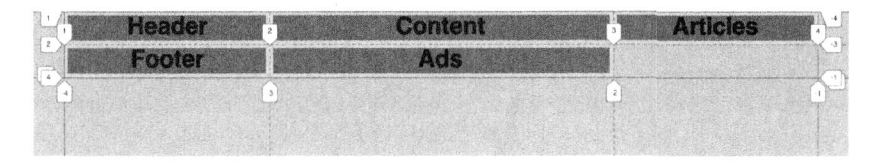

DEFINE THE GRID AREAS

It's now time to define the areas within the grid. Take a look at each cell in the mockup once again. As you can see, there are nine cells in a 3×3 grid. We're going to assign each one of these cells to an area with the grid-template-areas property.

- Let's edit the following CSS code:

```
.container {
display: grid;
grid-template-columns: 3fr 5fr 3fr;
grid-template-rows: auto auto auto;
grid-template-areas: "top top top" "left center right" "bottom bottom bottom";
}
```

The `grid-template-areas` property describes what the layout looks like in an easy to understand notation. You take each one of the cells per row in a grid and assign area names to them.

Notice that there are no commas separating the area names or at the end of each quoted row. There's a semicolon at the end of the declaration, as is normal in CSS. You can use whatever name you want to define these areas.

- You can now see the names of the areas you've defined inside the grid:

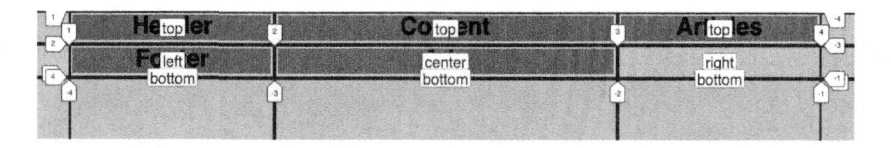

ASSIGN ITEMS TO THE GRID AREAS

Now let's place grid items inside the areas we've created.

- Edit the following CSS code:

```
.header {
grid-area: top;
}

.content {
grid-area: center;
}

.articles {
grid-area: right;
}

.footer {
grid-area: bottom;
}

.ads {
grid-area: left;
}
```

- You've just placed items inside the grid to the areas you've defined:

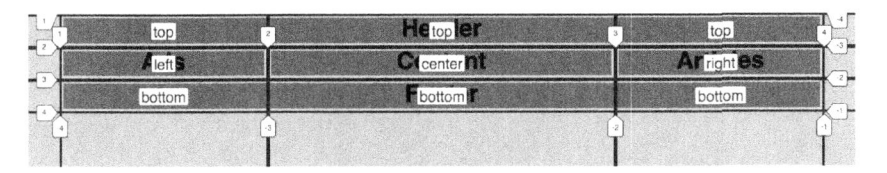

You can see that the browser shows the area names you've created. The grid items are nicely placed according to the template.

But what if you want to leave a blank space? For example, what happens if you don't want to assign a grid area to a particular cell? All you need to do is use a period. Notice the period at the end of this new CSS code:

```
.container {
```

```
display: grid;
grid-template-columns: 3fr 5fr 3fr;
grid-template-rows: auto auto auto;
grid-template-areas: "top top top" "left center right" "bottom bottom .";
}
```

- Here's how that CSS code will appear in your browser:

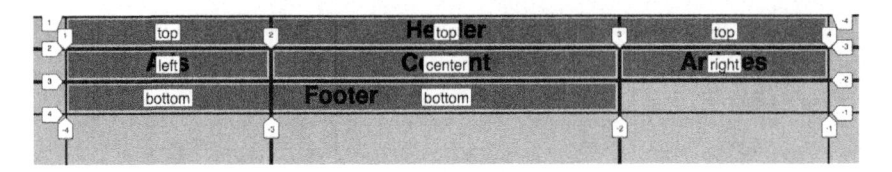

If you want to leave an empty cell, don't forget the period. The `grid-template-areas` property has to take each cell into account, otherwise you'll break the layout.

WORKING WITH MEDIA QUERIES

So far in this chapter, you've assigned each one of the items to their respective areas. The final step is to edit the `grid-template-areas` property to match the layout to different screen sizes:

- Add a media query to your CSS code:

```
/* Media Queries */
@media (min-width: 768px) and (max-width: 1024px) and (orientation: landscape)
{
.container {
grid-template-areas:
"left top top"
"left center center"
"bottom bottom right";
}
}
```

Your CSS Grid should now be responsive. Here is the layout on a small screen:

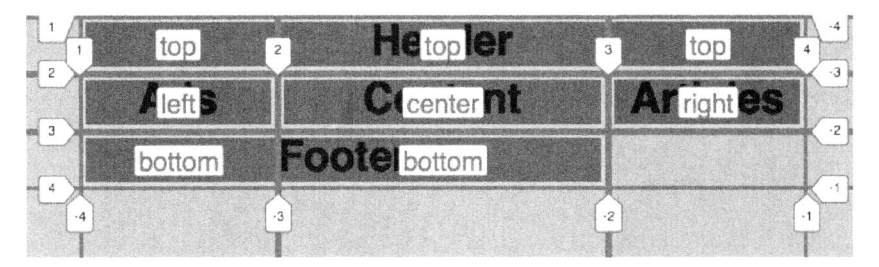

And here's the layout on a much larger screen:

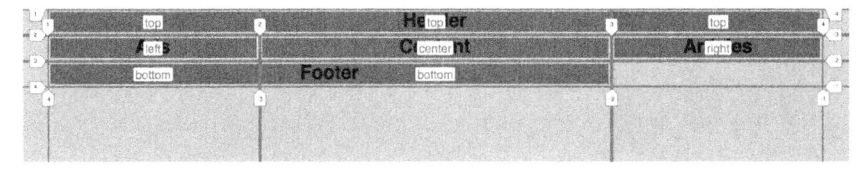

Now, its time for you to practice! Build your own layout with the grid-template-areas property and create a couple media queries to position elements inside those areas, changing the layout for each one of the device screen sizes.

CHAPTER 13.

HOW TO USE THE MINMAX() FUNCTION

The `minmax()` function is a very useful CSS Grid feature that allows you to specify the minimum and maximum sizes of a grid track.

One of the most popular uses of `minmax()` is creating responsive designs without the use of media queries. Thanks to CSS Grid and `minmax()`, you can do more with less and faster code.

Let's start by creating the HTML and CSS files.

You can find the code for this chapter at https://github.com/OSTraining/cssgrid/tree/master/minmax.

- Create a folder called /minmax/.
- Create an HTML file called minmax.html inside the folder.
- Enter this code:

```
<html>

<head>
<link     rel="stylesheet"      type="text/css" href="minmax.css">
</head>
```

```
<body>

<div class="container"</div>
<div class="item item1">First</div>
<div class="item item2">Second</div>
<div class="item item3">Third</div>
<div class="item item4">Fourth</div>
<div class="item item5">Fifth</div>
<div class="item item6">Sixth</div>
<div class="item item7">Seventh</div>
<div class="item item8">Eighth</div>
</div>

</body>

</html>
```

- Create a CSS file called minmax.css.
- Add the following styles:

```
/* GLOBAL STYLES */

* {
box-sizing: border-box;
}
body {
background-color: #AAA;margin: 50px;
}

/* Each item in the grid contains numbers */
.item {

/* Center the contents of the grid items. Making each grid item a Flex Container */
display: flex;

/* Horizontal and Vertical centering */
```

```
    justify-content: center;
    align-items: center;
    border: 5px solid #87b5ff;
    border-radius: 3px;
    font-size: 2em;
    font-family: sans-serif;
    font-weight: bold;
    background-color: #1c57b5;
}
```

When your code is correct, this is what you'll see when you open the minmax.html file in your browser:

CREATE THE GRID

Now, let's start the grid for this chapter. This grid will have three columns with the same width. The gap between columns and rows will be 20 px.

- Add this code to your CSS file:

```
/* CSS Grid Styles */
.container {
display: grid;
grid-template-columns: 1fr 1fr 1fr;
grid-gap: 2rem;
}
```

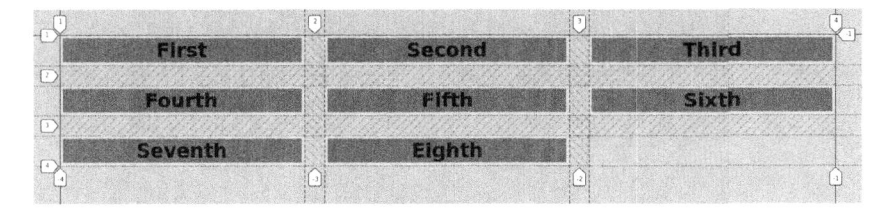

This grid is not responsive, but it is flexible.

- Resize the window of your browser. You will see that each column will shrink until it fits the widest content in that particular column. In the image below, I've circled the widest content in each column:

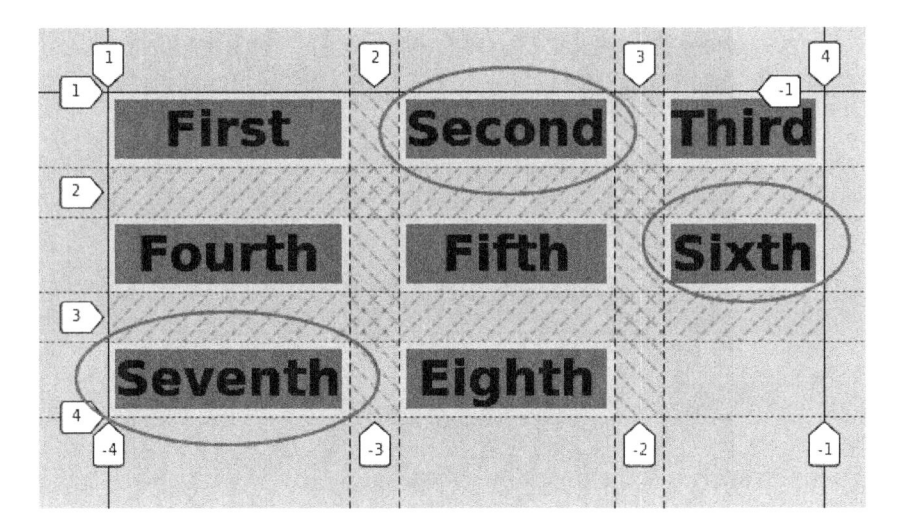

INTRODUCING MINMAX()

With the `minmax()` function, it's possible to set a range with the minimum and maximum size of a track. In this case we're using the function to define the column size.

- Update your CSS code to set the width of the first column to a minimum of 250px and a maximum of 480px:

```
.container {
```

```
display: grid;
grid-template-columns: minmax(250px, 480px) 1fr 1fr;
grid-gap: 2rem;
}
```

The first column is now 480px wide on a desktop screen. The second and third columns are set to 1fr. That means the second and third columns take up one fraction of the available remaining space each.

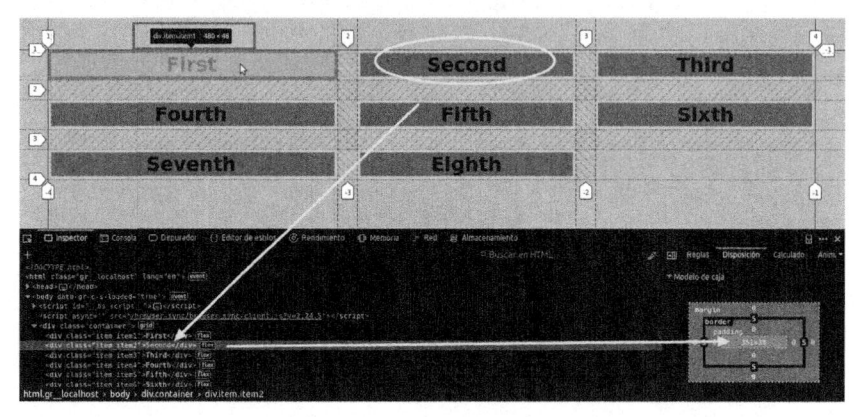

- Reduce the size of the browser window once again. Continue to reduce the size until the second and third columns have the value of `auto`, i.e. they are as wide as the widest content in them.

No matter how small you make the browser, the first column will keep a minimum width of 250px, as specified in the `minmax()` function.

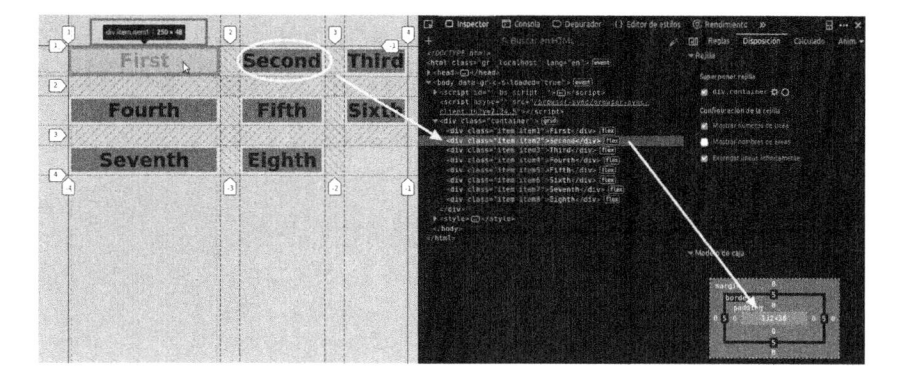

This example has shown you the basic functioning of `minmax()`.

There are two key rules to remember:

1. If the value of the `max` is less than the value of the `min`, the `max` will be ignored and the whole `minmax()` expression will be treated as the `min`.

2. It is not possible to set a flex value (fr units) as a minimum.

It's also worth noting that you can use the repeat notation to create patterns.

- Edit the CSS code:

```
.container {
display: grid;
grid-template-columns:   repeat(2,   minmax(80px,
160px) 1fr 2fr);
grid-gap: 2rem;
}
```

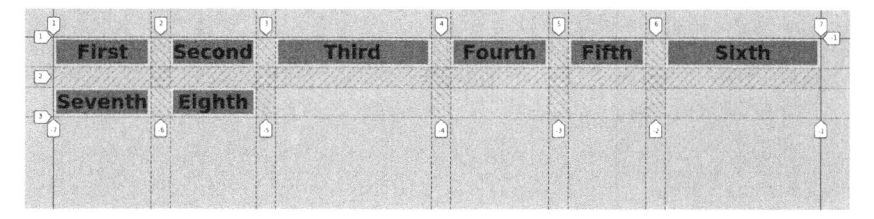

CSS GRID EXPLAINED 95

Thanks to this new code, the first, fourth, and seventh items are placed inside columns with fixed values. Those three columns have a minimum width of 80px and a maximum width of n160px.

- Resize the browser window. The content inside these columns will overflow its container, due to these fixed values.

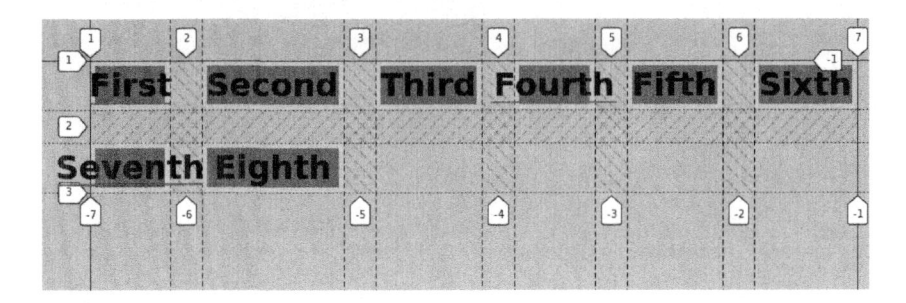

USING MINMAX() WITH ROWS

By default in CSS Grid, the height of each row is set to auto. These rows are as high as the content inside them.

However, you may need to have rows in a grid with a predefined height. This means that the rows have a minimum height, independently from the content inside them.

The `minmax()` function allows you to set a minimum row height, when used inside the `grid-template-rows` property.

- Edit the CSS code:

```
/* CSS Grid Styles */
.container {
display: grid;
grid-template-columns: 1fr 1fr 1fr;
grid-template-rows:    repeat(3,   minmax(75px, auto));
```

```
grid-gap: 2rem;
}
```

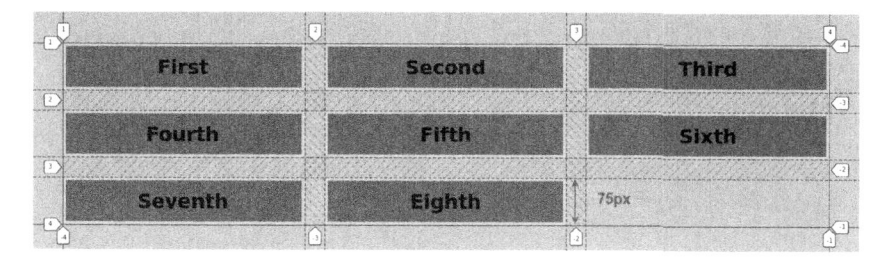

[Figure showing a grid with three rows and three columns containing items First, Second, Third, Fourth, Fifth, Sixth, Seventh, Eighth, with a 75px row height indicator]

Now the grid has three rows. The rows have a minimum height of 75px. The maximum height of these rows will be determined by the content inside each of the items.

- Edit the HTML code to illustrate this:

```
<div class="container">
<div class="item item1">First</div>
<div class="item item2">Second</div>
<div class="item item3">Third</div>
<div class="item item4">Fourth</div>
<div class="item item5"><blockquote>minmax(min, max)Defines a size range greater than or equal to min and less than or equal to max
</div>
<div class="item item6">Sixth</div>
<div class="item item7">Seventh</div>
<div class="item item8">Eighth</div>
</div>
```

The second row is now as high as the content in it. The other two rows have a height of 75px.

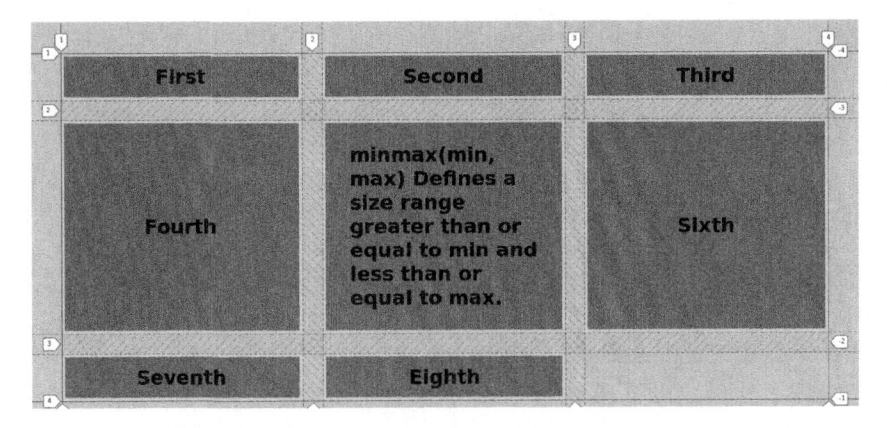

First	Second	Third
Fourth	minmax(min, max) Defines a size range greater than or equal to min and less than or equal to max.	Sixth
Seventh	Eighth	

So to summarize this chapter, the `minmax()` function allows you to specify a minimum and maximum size in CSS Grid. This allows you to set a range for the width and height of CSS Grid columns and rows. In many situations, you can use `minmax()` instead of media queries.

In the next chapter, we're going to build on the `minmax()` function and combine it with two very useful keywords.

CHAPTER 14.

HOW TO USE THE AUTO-FILL AND AUTO-FIT KEYWORDS

In earlier chapters, we've seen that CSS Grid allows us to create repeating track patterns.

However, using this method gives you a fixed number of tracks, independently of the content inside each one of them.

The `auto-fill` and `auto-fit` keywords will allow you to place as many tracks of the specified size as possible, depending on the size of the viewport.

CREATE THE HTML AND CSS

You'll find the code for this chapter on Github: https://github.com/OSTraining/cssgrid/tree/master/auto-fill.

- Create a folder called /auto-fill/.
- Create an HTML file called auto-fill.html inside the folder.
- Enter this code:

```
<html>

<head>
<link         rel="stylesheet"         type="text/css"
```

```html
          href="auto-fill.css">
</head>

<body>

<div class="container">
<div class="item item1">First</div>
<div class="item item2">Second</div>
<div class="item item3">Third</div>
<div class="item item4">Fourth</div>
<div class="item item5">Fifth</div>
<div class="item item6">Sixth</div>
<div class="item item7">Seventh</div>
<div class="item item8">Eighth</div>
</div>

</body>

</html>
```

- Create a CSS file called auto-fill.css.
- Add the following styles:

```css
/* GLOBAL STYLES */
* {
box-sizing: border-box;
}

body {
background-color: #AAA;margin: 50px;
}
/* Each item in the grid contains numbers */
.item {
/* Center the contents of the grid items. Making each grid item a Flex Container */
display: flex;
/* Horizontal and Vertical centering */
```

```
justify-content: center;
align-items: center;
border: 5px solid #87b5ff;
border-radius: 3px;
font-size: 2em;
font-family: sans-serif;
font-weight: bold;
background-color: #1c57b5;
}
```

CREATE THE CSS GRID

Now let's create a grid with four columns. Each column will have a width of 200px and there will be a 1.5rem gap between the columns and rows of 1.5rem.

```
/* CSS Grid styles */
.container {
display: grid;
grid-template-columns: repeat(4, 200px);
grid-gap: 1.5rem;
}
```

This image shows how your grid should look:

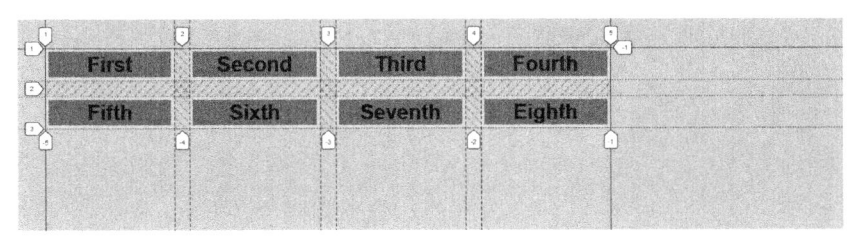

As you can see, there's room on the right of the grid container. We could place the fifth item on the first row. However, we already declared four columns, so this extra space on desktop screens isn't used.

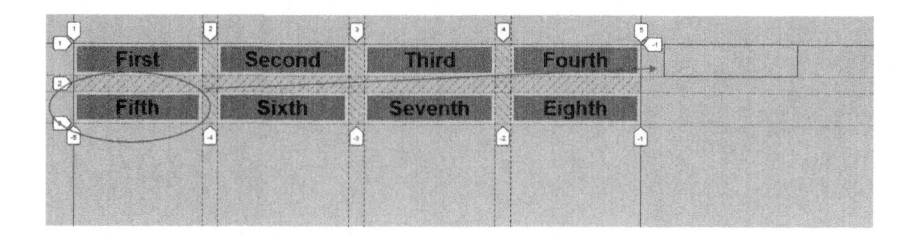

THE AUTO-FILL AND AUTO-FIT KEYWORDS

Let's move away from the four column layout. We're still using the repeat notation, but now we're using auto-fill to create as many columns as the browser will allow.

- Update your CSS with this code:

```
.container {
display: grid;
grid-template-columns: repeat(auto-fill, 200px);
grid-gap: 1.5rem;
}
```

The grid container is now wide enough to hold five items, each one with a width of 200px:

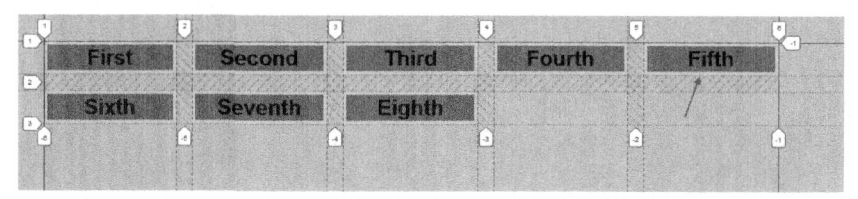

- Resize the browser window, in order to make it narrower, for example to 800px

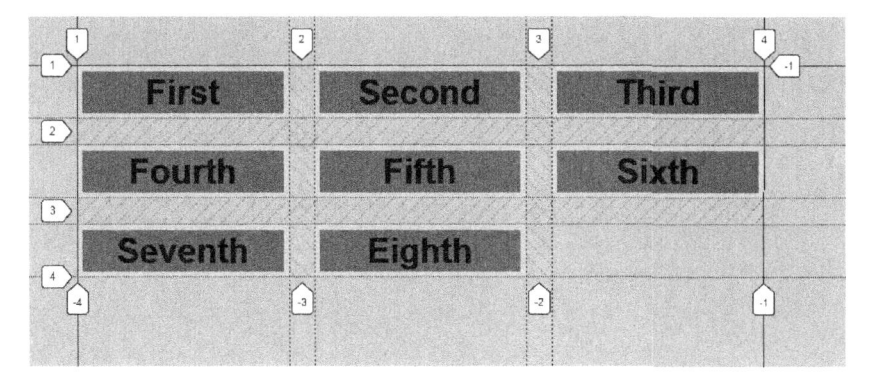

[Grid diagram showing First, Second, Third / Fourth, Fifth, Sixth / Seventh, Eighth]

The fourth and fifth items wrapped over to the next row, because there is room for only three columns now. This is the math:

3 columns (200px each) = 600px

Gap between columns = 24px * 2= 48px

Total space in use = 648px

Viewport width = 800px

Available remaining space = 800px − 648px = 152px

The fourth item wraps to the next column because it's not possible to create a 200px column to the right, there's no space for it.

- Edit the CSS code once again:

```
.container {
display: grid;
grid-template-columns: repeat(auto-fit, 200px);
grid-gap: 1.5rem;
}
```

You won't see any change in the layout.

In order to illustrate the difference between `auto-fill` and `auto-fit`, edit the HTML code and remove Items 4 to 7:

```
<div class="container">
<div class="item item1">First</div>
<div class="item item2">Second</div>
<div class="item item3">Third</div>
</div>
```

These two images show the difference between `auto-fill` and `auto-fit`:

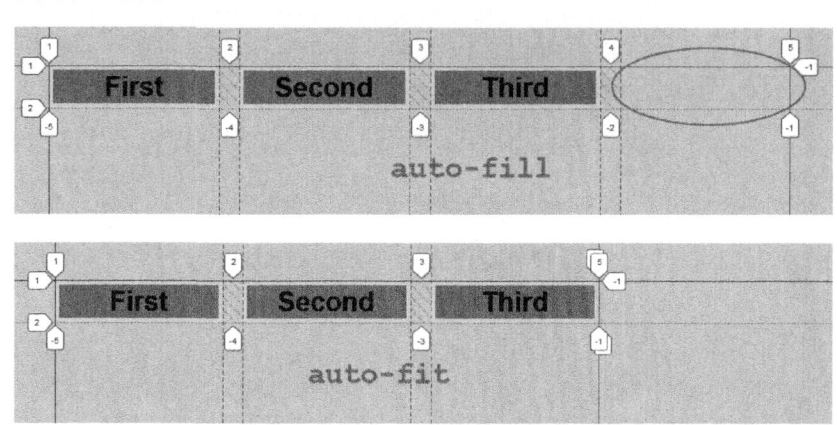

- Update your CSS with this code:

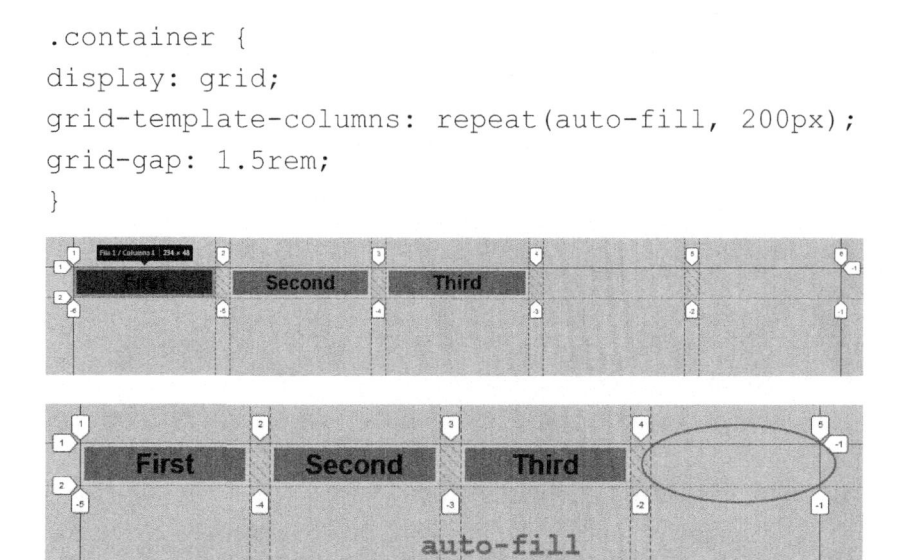

```
.container {
display: grid;
grid-template-columns: repeat(auto-fill, 200px);
grid-gap: 1.5rem;
}
```

The `auto-fill` creates additional empty columns if there's space available. The `auto-fit` ends the grid container with the last grid item, independently if there's room for another column.

That means you could span Item 3 across two columns or even place one of the items on the last cell of that row, if you're using `auto-fill`, for example.

You might be thinking that this is somehow practical, but it's not really useful. Read on, in order to discover the real power of these keywords.

USING AUTO-FILL AND AUTO-FIT WITH MINMAX()

We saw in the last chapter that the `minmax()` function in CSS allows you to specify the minimum and maximum sizes of a grid track. Using `minmax()` together with `auto-fill` or `auto-fit` gives you the ability to create a grid with responsive behavior.

- Edit the following CSS code:

```
.container {
display: grid;
grid-template-columns:          repeat(auto-fill, 
minmax(200px, 1fr));
grid-gap: 1.5rem;
}
```

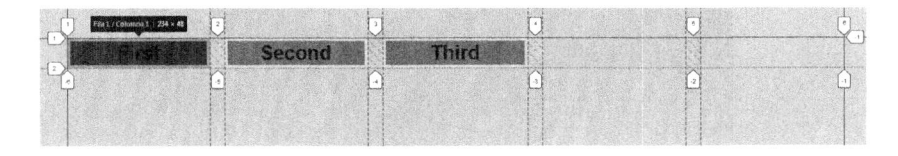

The `auto-fill` places two additional columns according to the available viewport space. However, the size of these columns is not fixed.

It is a fraction of the available space, so it will adjust the size of the columns based on the values specified as parameters within the minmax() function.

- Resize your viewport until you see the third item wrap over to the next row:

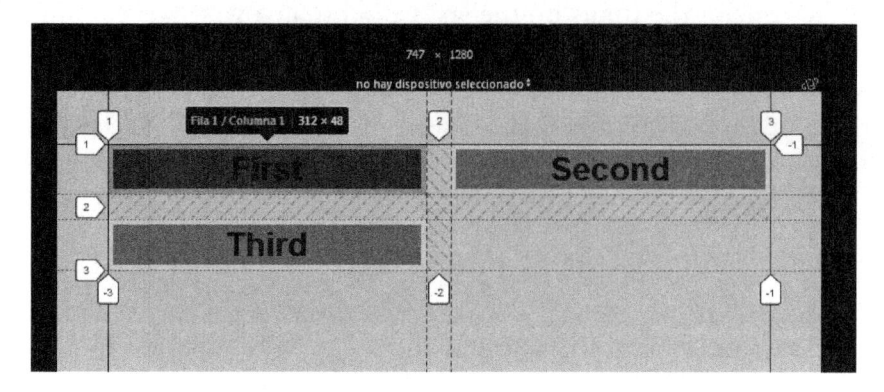

Let's see what happens with the `auto-fit` keyword!

- Edit the following CSS code:

```
.container {
display: grid;
grid-template-columns:          repeat(auto-fit,
minmax(200px, 1fr));
grid-gap: 1.5rem;
}
```

All columns are evenly distributed across the available viewport space. If you resize the viewport to 524px, you will see how the third column wraps over to the next row.

Here's the math:

2 columns (200px each) = 400px – the minimum size according to minmax()

Gap between columns = 24px

Total space in use = 424px

Body margin (set in the global styles) = 50px to left and right = 100px

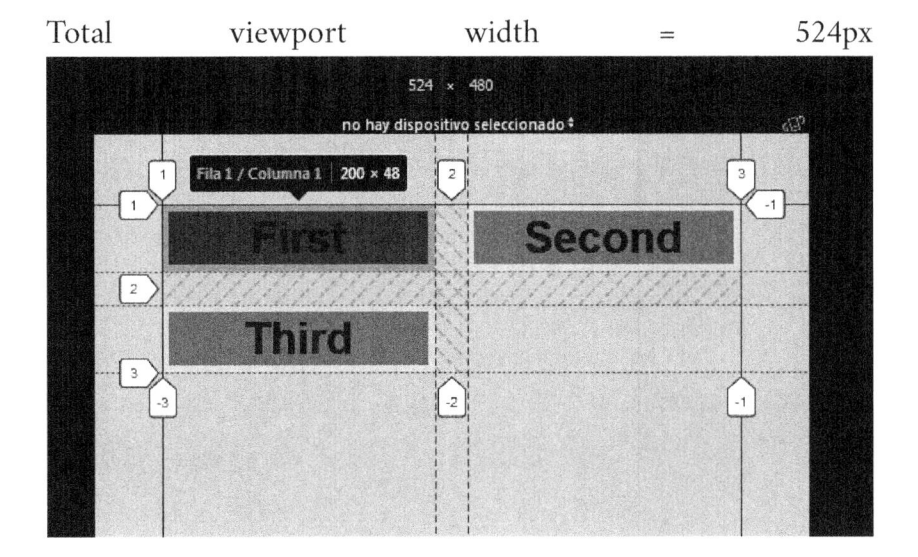

Total viewport width = 524px

Now you have a flexible grid with responsive behavior without the need of writing media queries or adding extra classes (for example, Bootstrap classes) to the items in the markup.

You can see now how useful the `auto-fill` and `auto-fit` keywords in CSS Grid are. They really help you create flexible and responsive grids.

CHAPTER 15.

THE GRID-AUTO-FLOW: DENSE PROPERTY

You have learned that CSS Grid uses a row-based flow to place items inside a grid.

In CSS Grid, items automatically wrap over to the next row and are placed into grid areas if there's enough space available. If there's not enough space, the item will jump over to the next slot where it can fit.

This can lead to a grid layout with empty spaces because the placement algorithm is placing the grid items according to a sequence. The `grid-auto-flow: dense` property will allow you to fill those empty spaces with grid items of the right size, independently of the source order of the document.

Let's demonstrate this property with an example!

CREATE THE HTML AND CSS

The code for this chapter is available here: https://github.com/OSTraining/cssgrid/tree/master/grid-auto-flow.

- Create a folder called /grid-auto-flow/.
- Create an HTML file called grid-auto-flow.html inside the folder.
- Enter this code:

```html
<html>

<head>
<link    rel="stylesheet"    type="text/css" href="grid-auto-flow.css">
</head>

<body>

<div class="container"</div>
<div class="item item1">1</div>
<div class="item item2">2</div>
<div class="item item3">3</div>
<div class="item item4">4</div>
<div class="item item5">5</div>
<div class="item item6">6</div>
<div class="item item7">7</div>
<div class="item item8">8</div>
<div class="item item9">9</div>
<div class="item item10">10</div>
<div class="item item11">11</div>
<div class="item item12">12</div>
<div class="item item13">13</div>
<div class="item item14">14</div>
<div class="item item15">15</div>
<div class="item item16">16</div>
<div class="item item17">17</div>
<div class="item item18">18</div>
<div class="item item19">19</div>
<div class="item item20">20</div>
<div class="item item21">21</div>
<div class="item item22">22</div>
<div class="item item23">23</div>
<div class="item item24">24</div>
<div class="item item25">25</div>
</div>
```

```
</body>

</html>
```

Create the global styles for the markup you just created:

- Create a CSS file called grid-auto-flow.css.
- Add the following styles:

```
/* GLOBAL STYLES */
* {
box-sizing: border-box;
}

body {
background-color: #AAA;
margin: 50px;
}

/* Each item in the grid contains numbers */
.item {
/* Center the contents of the grid items, making
each grid item a Flex Container */
display: flex;

/* Horizontal and Vertical centering */
justify-content: center;
align-items: center;
border: 5px solid #87b5ff;
border-radius: 3px;
font-size: 2em;
font-family: sans-serif;
font-weight: bold;
background-color: #1c57b5;
}
```

CREATE THE CSS GRID

For this chapter, we're going to create a grid with five columns and five rows. The height of each one of the elements will be auto (default).

You'll be changing the size of a couple of them, in order to generate blank spaces within the grid. The gap between columns and rows will be 2em, that's about 32px on a desktop screen.

- Add this code to your CSS file:

```
.container {
display: grid;
grid-template-columns: repeat(5, 1fr);
grid-template-rows: repeat(5, 1fr);
grid-gap: 2em;
}
```

This is the normal flow of the grid. The browser takes each item and places it from left to right and from top to bottom, like in western languages, according to CSS Grid's placement algorithm.

CHANGING THE SIZE OF SOME GRID ITEMS

We need to change the size of some of the items, in order to make some blank spaces appear on the grid.

The CSS `:nth-child` pseudo-class will allow us to target specific items, more precisely each third, fifth, and seventh item in the source order.

- Add this new CSS code:

```
.item:nth-child(3n) {
grid-column: span 4;
background-color: #12cc12;
}

.item:nth-child(5n) {
grid-column: span 3;
background-color: #f5ecec;
}

.item:nth-child(7n) {
grid-column: span 2;
background-color: #f35810;
}
```

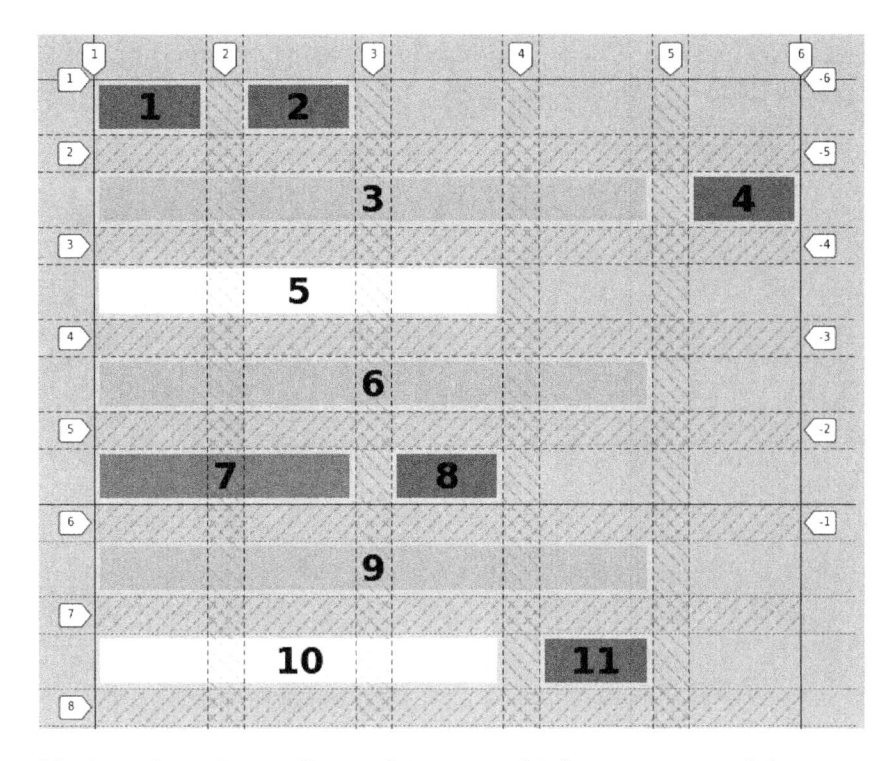

Notice that the styling of items, which are targeted by two different CSS pseudo-classes (i.e. Items 15 and 21), will be ruled by the last available selector in the source order of the CSS code. Moreover, the grid items have been placed on the implicit grid from Item 9 onwards.

As you can see, Item 3, for example, does not fit into the available space on the first row. So Item 3 wraps over to the next row, leaving three empty grid cells on that row. Item 4 comes after

CSS GRID EXPLAINED 113

Item 3 according to the source order of the markup.

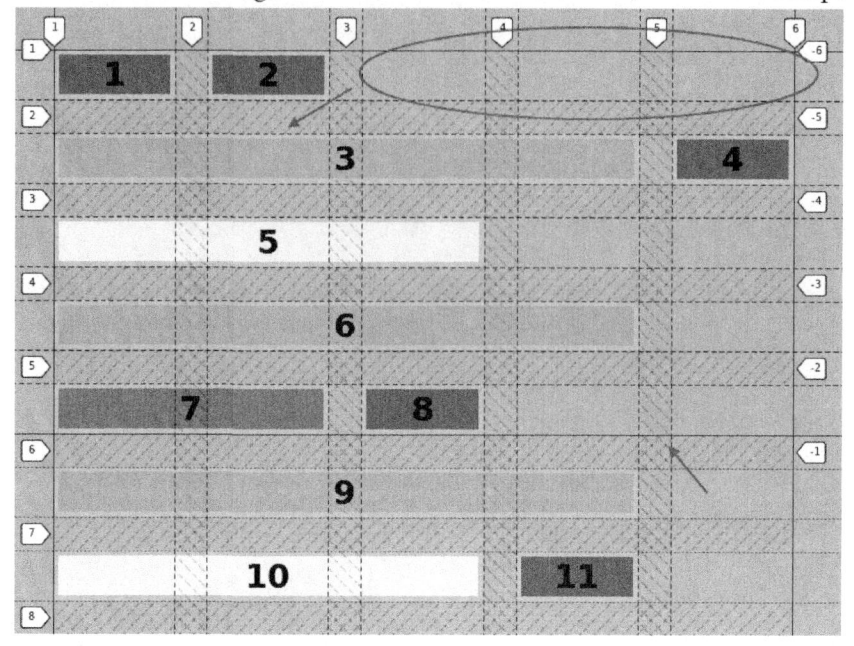

THE GRID-AUTO-FLOW: DENSE PROPERTY

It's time to use the grid-auto-flow: dense property, which will place items on the grid, according to their size, making use of that available empty space.

- Update your CSS code

```
.container {
display: grid;
grid-template-columns: repeat(5, 5fr);
grid-template-rows: repeat(5, 5fr);
grid-gap: 2em;
grid-auto-flow: dense;
}
```

Now you can see that Item 4 has taken the available space on the first row between lines #3 and #4, Item 7 has been placed with the same logic and so on. This is very useful if the source order of the markup is not relevant to the presentation layer, for example with an image gallery.

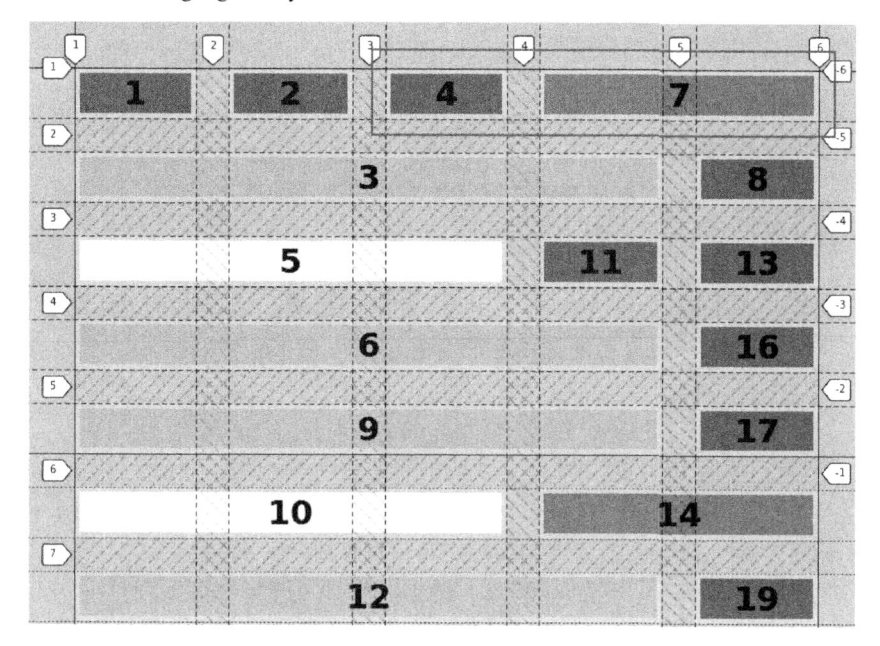

As already stated, the default flow of the grid is the row. So, if you edit the CSS code and add the keyword row to the grid-auto-flow property, you won't see any difference.

- Update your CSS code:

```
.container {
display: grid;
grid-template-columns: repeat(5, 5fr);
grid-template-rows: repeat(5, 5fr);
grid-gap: 2em;
grid-auto-flow: row dense;
}
```

- Edit the CSS code once again to test the column auto-flow property:

```
.container {
display: grid;
```

```
grid-template-columns: repeat(5, 5fr);
grid-template-rows: repeat(5, 5fr);
grid-gap: 2em;
grid-auto-flow: column dense;
}
```

Now items flow from top to bottom and then from left to right in a column-based flow. The width of items that haven't been spanned has become auto, and the explicit grid ends with Item 13.

The `grid-auto-flow` property takes control over the functioning of the placement algorithm for the items onto the grid. The dense keyword places items on blank spaces of the grid, according to their size.

This is very useful if you don't have to preserve the source order of the markup within the visual presentation of your site.

CHAPTER 16.

HOW TO ALIGN ITEMS IN CSS GRID

In the last few chapters, we looked at how to create flexible layouts in CSS Grid. We're now going to turn our attention to aligning items within a grid.

CSS Grid Layout is a two dimensional layout model.

This means it operates with two axes: the block axis, also known as the y-axis and the inline axis, also known as the x-axis.

When dealing with the block axis (vertical), you'll be using the `align` property, whereas if you want to align or center on the horizontal axis, you should use the `justify` property.

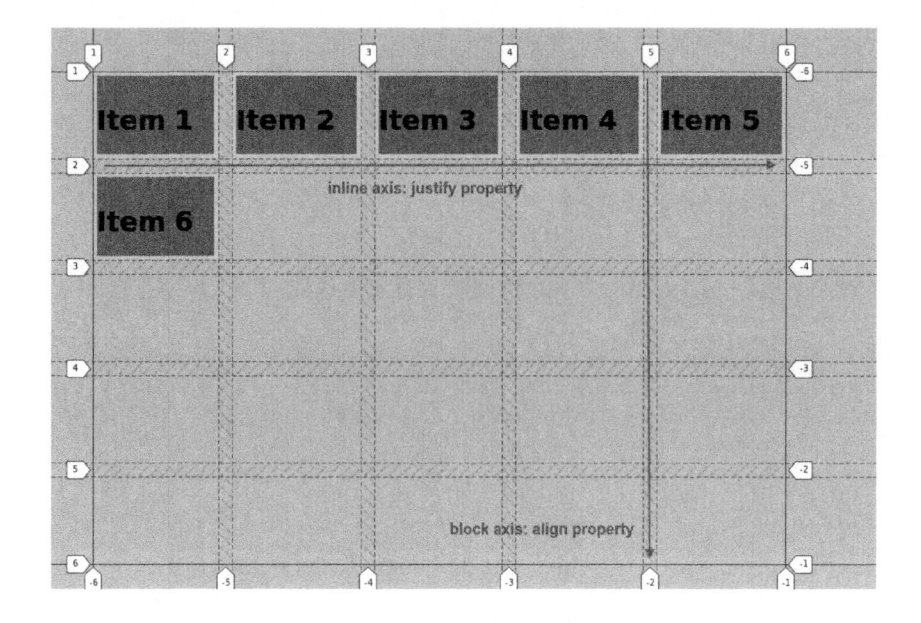

CREATE THE HTML AND CSS

You can download the code for this chapter on Github: https://github.com/OSTraining/cssgrid/tree/master/align-items.

- Create a folder called /align-items/.
- Create an HTML file called align-items.html inside the folder.
- Enter this code:

```
<html>

<head>
<link       rel="stylesheet"       type="text/css"
href="align-items.css">
</head>

<body>
<div class="container">
<div class="item item1">Item 1</div>
```

```
<div class="item item2">Item 2</div>
<div class="item item3">Item 3</div>
<div class="item item4">Item 4</div>
<div class="item item5">Item 5</div>
<div class="item item6">Item 6</div>
</div>

</body>

</html>
```

- Create a CSS file called align-items.css.
- Add the following styles:

```
/* GLOBAL STYLES */

* {
box-sizing: border-box;
}

body {
background-color: #AAA;
margin: 50px;
}

.item {
border: 5px solid #87b5ff;
border-radius: 3px;
font-size: 2em;
font-family: sans-serif;
font-weight: bold;
background-color: #1c57b5
}
```

CREATE THE CSS GRID

Create a grid with five columns and five rows. Each column will have a width of 150px and each row will have a height of 100px. The gap between columns and rows will be 1rem (that is about 16px in a desktop screen).

```
.container {
display: grid;
grid-gap: 1rem;
grid-template-columns: repeat(5, 150px);
grid-template-rows: repeat(5, 100px);
}
```

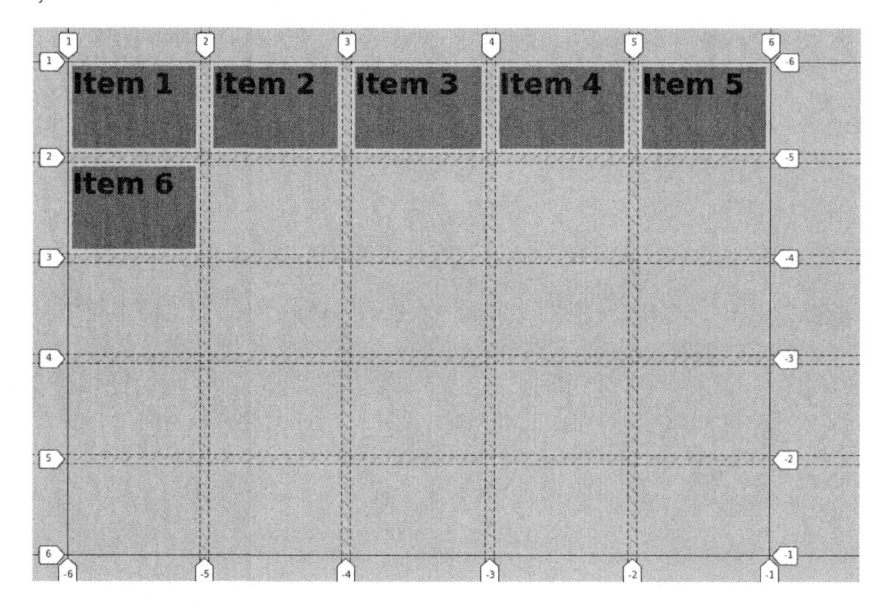

Now, place the items on different areas of the grid with help of the `grid-column` and `grid-row` properties and the numbered lines in the grid.

- Add this new CSS code:

```
.item1 {
grid-row: 1 / 3;
}

.item2 {
```

```
grid-column: 2 / 4;
}

.item3 {
grid-row: 1 / 4;
grid-column: 4 / 5;
}

.item4 {
grid-row: 2 / -2;
grid-column: 5 / -1;
}

.item5 {
grid-row: 4 / -1;
grid-column: 2 / 4;
}

.item6 {
grid-row: 3 / -1;
}
```

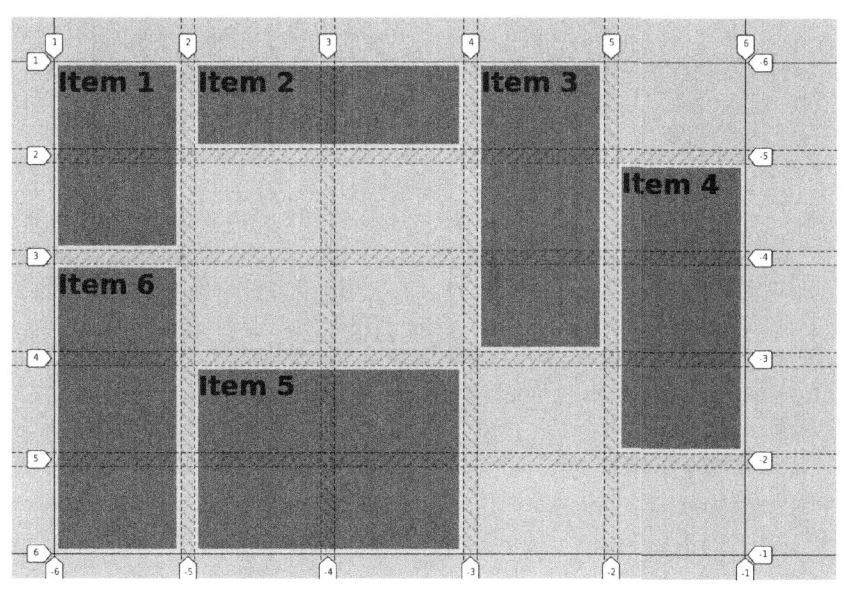

THE ALIGN-ITEMS PROPERTY

This property is used at the grid container level. As already stated, the `align` deals with the vertical (block) axis.

- Update your CSS code for the container div:

```
.container {
display: grid;
grid-gap: 1rem;
grid-template-columns: repeat(5, 150px);
grid-template-rows: repeat(5, 100px);
align-items: center;
}
```

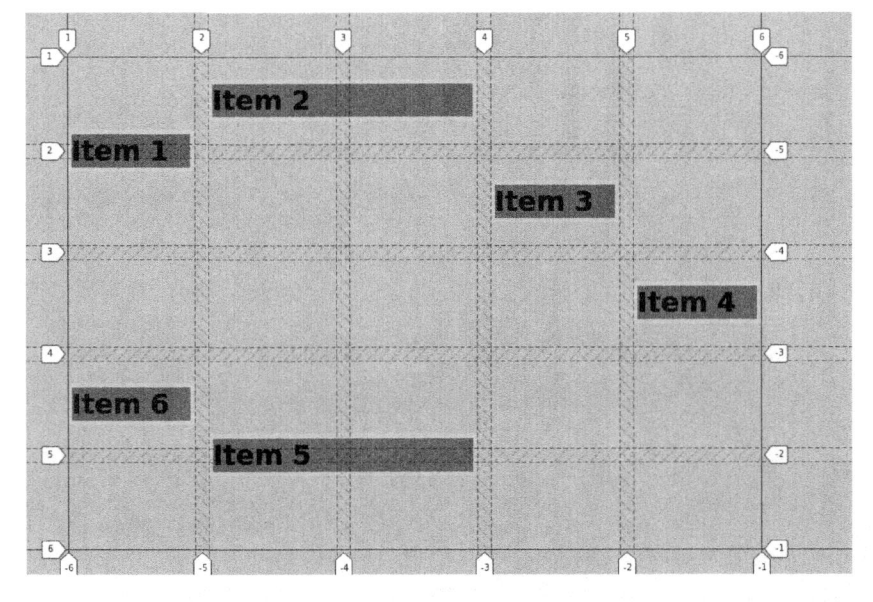

As you can see, now all items have a height value of `auto`. This means they are as tall as the content inside them.

All items are vertically centered within their respective grid area (the ones you defined by placing grid items with line numbers).

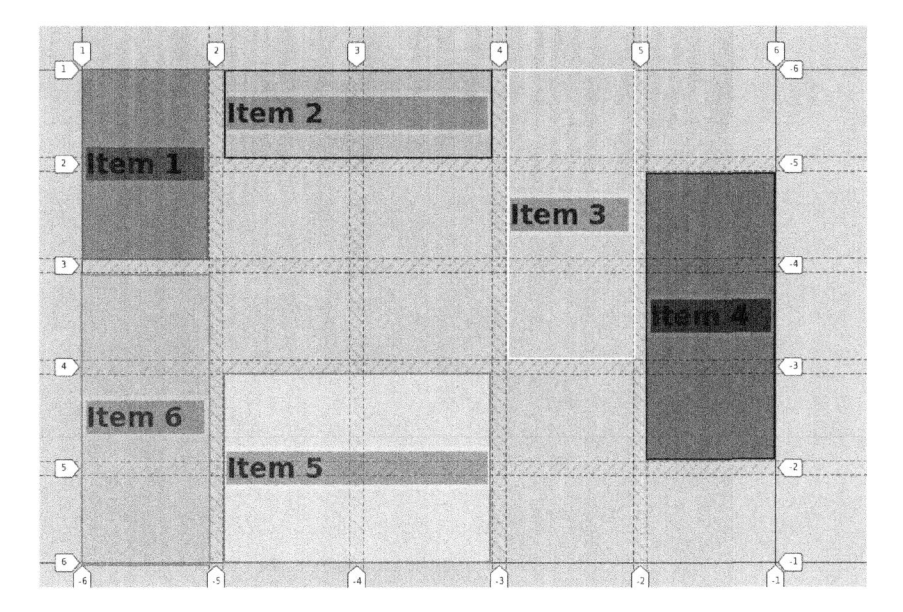

These are some of the values you can pass to the align-items property:

- start
- end
- stretch

Update the CSS code again, in order to test these values:

```
.container {
display: grid;
grid-gap: 1rem;
grid-template-columns: repeat(5, 150px);
grid-template-rows: repeat(5, 100px);
align-items: start;
}
```

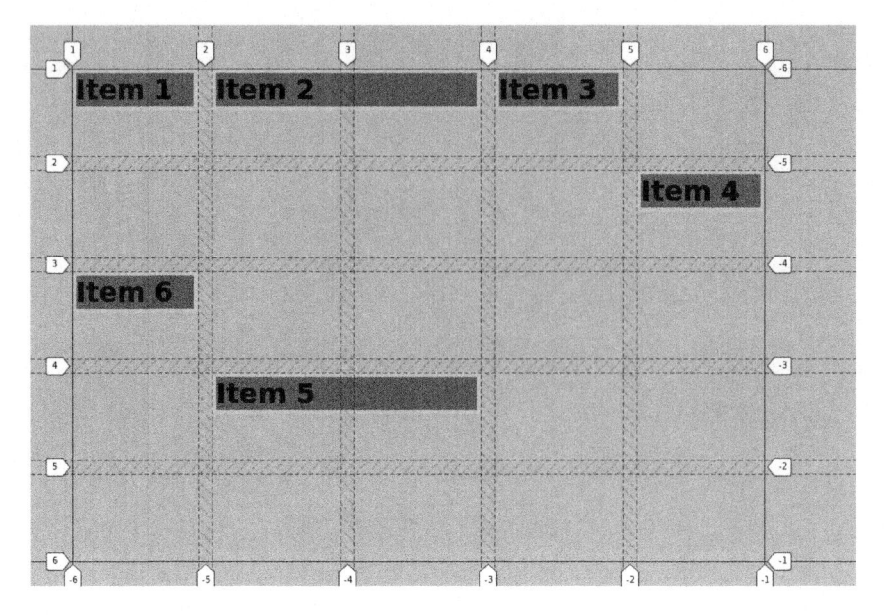

Each item is now placed at the start of its corresponding grid area.

Setting the value of the `align-items` property to `end` will place the items (vertically) to the end of their corresponding grid areas.

The value assigned to the `stretch` will stretch the items across the whole area.

Update the CSS code once again:

```
.container {
display: grid;
grid-gap: 1rem;
grid-template-columns: repeat(5, 150px);
grid-template-rows: repeat(5, 100px);
align-items: stretch;
}
```

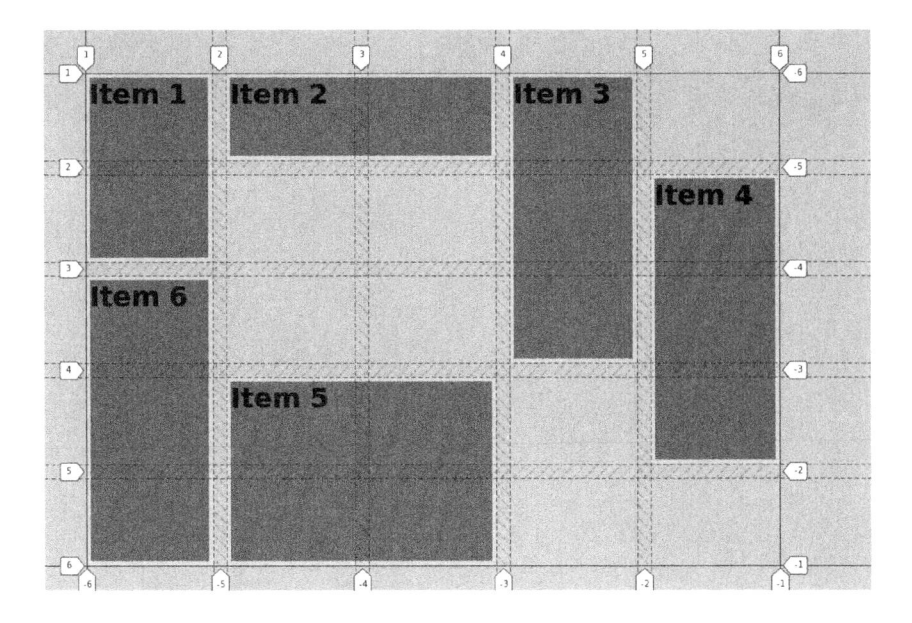

THE JUSTIFY-ITEMS PROPERTY

The `justify-items` property accepts the same values and works pretty much the same as the `align-items` property but on the inline (horizontal) axis.

- Update your container div CSS again:

```
.container {
display: grid;
grid-gap: 1rem;
grid-template-columns: repeat(5, 150px);
grid-template-rows: repeat(5, 100px);
align-items: center;
justify-items: center;
}
```

As you can notice, the items are now as high and as wide as the content inside of them. Moreover, they are perfectly placed in the center of their respective grid areas.

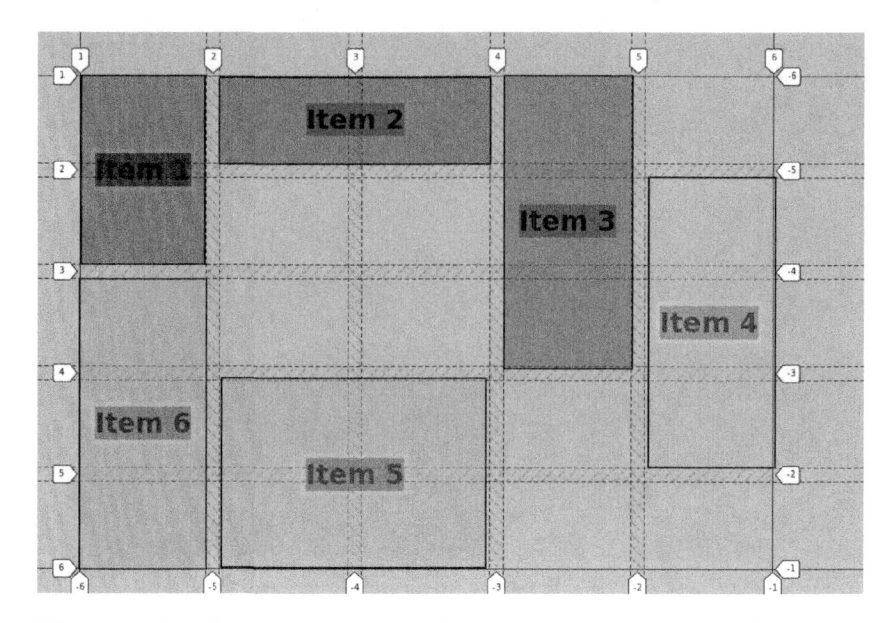

This is the basic usage of the justify-items and align-items properties.

But what if you want to target just one item, in order to align and/or center it? For those cases, you should use the align-self and justify-self properties at the item level.

THE ALIGN-SELF AND JUSTIFY-SELF PROPERTIES

These properties are used at the item level.

- Update your CSS code:

```
.item2 {
grid-column: 2 / 4;
justify-self: stretch;
}

.item3 {
grid-row: 1 / 4;
grid-column: 4 / 5;
```

```
align-self: stretch;
}

.item4 {
grid-row: 2 / -2;
grid-column: 5 / -1;
align-self: end;
}
```

Item 2 stretches across the whole grid area along its horizontal axis (justify).

Item 3 stretches vertically along the block axis and Item 4 has been placed vertically to the end of its grid area.

The other Items (1, 5 and 6) are placed according to the properties declared at the grid container level.

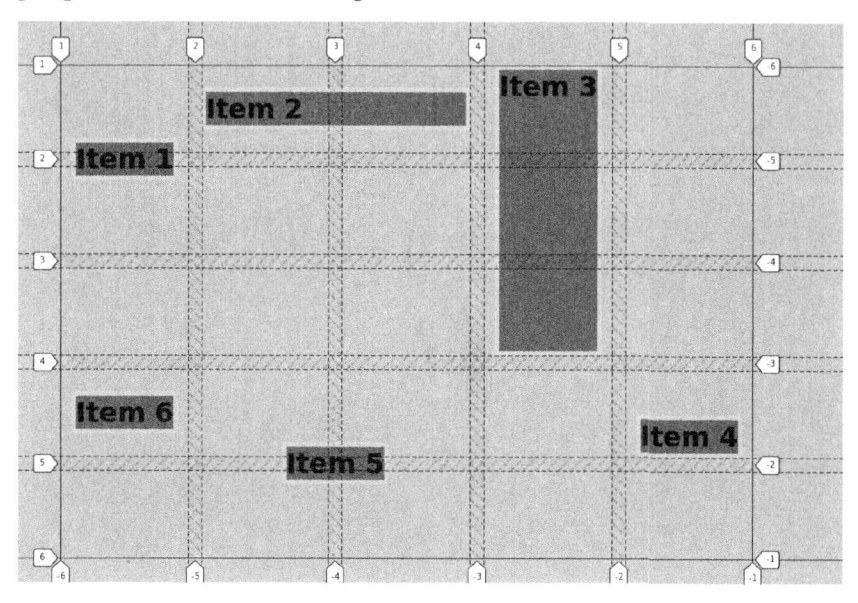

The `align` and `justify` properties allow you to center and align items relative to their containing grid area. These properties allow this in a comprehensive way with less code than trying to align the items with other layout methods.

In the next chapter, we'll explore the `align` and `justify` properties in more detail.

CHAPTER 17.

THE JUSTIFY-CONTENT AND ALIGN-CONTENT PROPERTIES

In the last chapter, you learned about the `align-content` and `justify-content` properties. These allow you to center and align items within a grid on the horizontal and vertical axes.

However, there are cases in which the total size of the grid is less than the size of the grid container. This happens because all items within the grid and the container itself are sized with fixed values (px, em, rem).

In these cases, we have to align the tracks themselves, that is the whole grid. This enables us to exploit and fill up that additional empty space. In such a situation, you can make use of the `align-content` and `justify-content` properties. This is what we'll look at in this chapter.

CREATE THE HTML AND CSS

You can find the code for this chapter on Github: https://github.com/OSTraining/cssgrid/tree/master/justify-content.

- Create a folder called /auto-fill/.

- Create an HTML file called justify-content.html inside the folder.
- Enter this code:

```html
<html>

<head>
<link         rel="stylesheet"         type="text/css" href="justify-content.css">
</head>

<body>

<div class="container">
<div class="item item1">1</div>
<div class="item item2">2</div>
<div class="item item3">3</div>
<div class="item item4">4</div>
<div class="item item5">5</div>
</div>

</body>

</html>
```

- Create a CSS file called justify-content.css.
- Add the following styles:

```css
/* GLOBAL STYLES */
* {
* {
box-sizing: border-box;
}

body {
background-color: #AAA;
```

```
  margin: 50px;
}

/* Each item in the grid contains numbers */
.item {
/* Center the contents of the grid items. Making
each grid item a Flex Container */
display: flex;

/* Horizontal and Vertical centering */
justify-content: center;
align-items: center;
border: 5px;
border-radius: 3px;
font-size: 2em;
font-family: sans-serif;
font-weight: bold;
}
```

CREATE THE CSS GRID

Create a grid with three columns and two rows. The first and third columns will have a width of 120px. The second column will have a width of 180px. The gap between columns will be set to 2rem, that's about 32px on a desktop screen. Each row will have a height of 80px.

The grid container itself will have a width of 900px and a height of 450px.

```
/* CSS Grid Styles */
```

```
.container {
display: grid;
border: 4px solid #fff;
width: 900px;
height: 450px;
grid-template-columns: 120px 180px 120px;
grid-template-rows: 80px 80px;
grid-gap: 2rem;
}
```

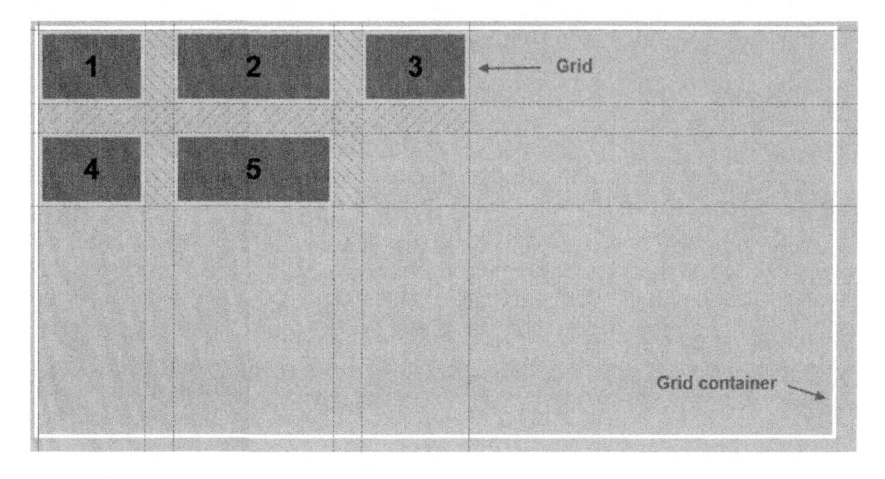

As you can see, the grid container is wider and taller than the grid itself. The `justify-content` and `align-content` properties are used to distribute and/or align all grid items (the tracks) within the grid container. Let's take a look at the possible values for these properties.

THE JUSTIFY-CONTENT AND ALIGN-CONTENT PROPERTIES

- Update your CSS code:

```
.container {
display: grid;
border: 4px solid #fff;
width: 900px;
```

```
height: 450px;
grid-template-columns: 120px 180px 120px;
grid-template-rows: 80px 80px;
grid-gap: 2rem;
justify-content: start;
align-content: start;
}
```

You will see no difference when refreshing your browser tab, and that's because the default value for these two properties is `start`.

Let's move the grid on the horizontal axis.

- Update your CSS code:

```
.container {
display: grid;
border: 4px solid #fff;
width: 900px;
height: 450px;
grid-template-columns: 120px 180px 120px;
grid-template-rows: 80px 80px;
grid-gap: 2rem;
justify-content: center;
align-content: start;
}
```

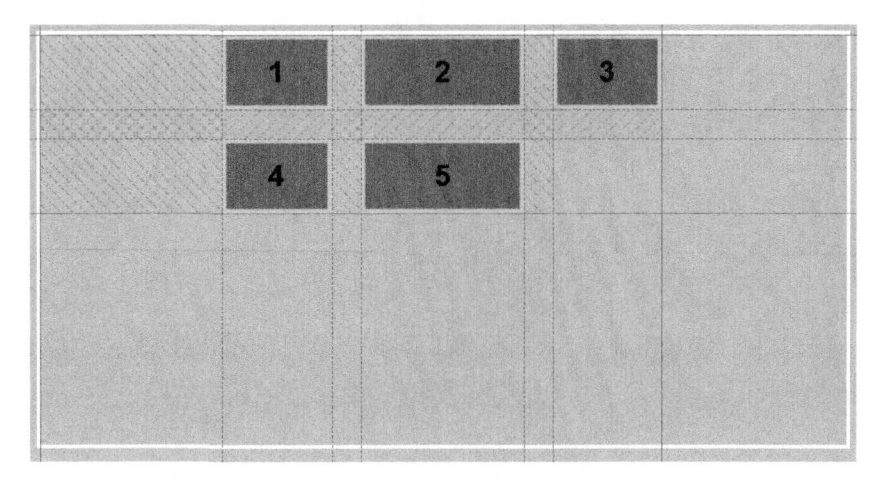

The whole grid has now moved to the center of its container on the horizontal axis. Let's try the vertical axis.

- Update the CSS code:

```
.container {
display: grid;
border: 4px solid #fff;
width: 900px;
height: 450px;
grid-template-columns: 120px 180px 120px;
grid-template-rows: 80px 80px;
grid-gap: 2rem;
justify-content: center;
align-content: end;
}
```

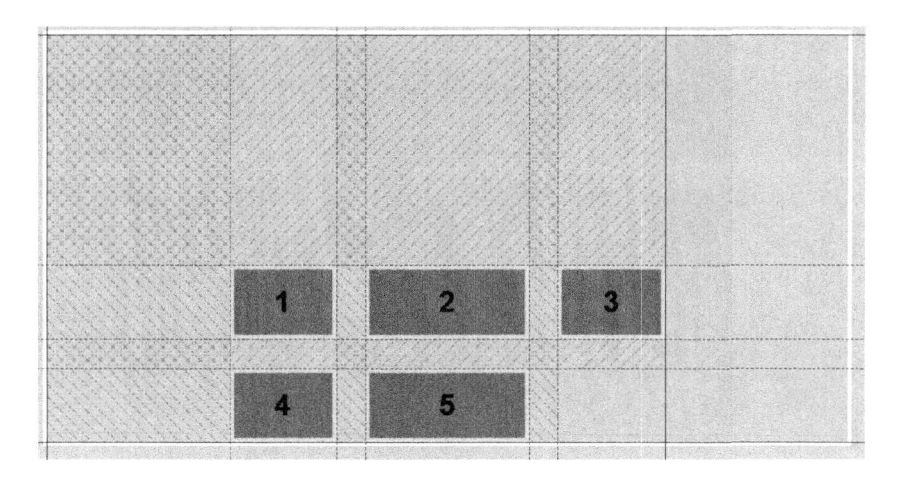

By now you already know how to center the whole grid within its container. But what if you want to distribute all grid tracks over the whole grid container? There are three additional values that will help you achieve this:

- `space-around`
- `space-between`
- `space-evenly`

Let's see them in action.

- Edit the CSS code in order to test these values:

```
.container {
display: grid;
border: 4px solid #fff;
width: 900px;
height: 450px;
grid-template-columns: 120px 180px 120px;
grid-template-rows: 80px 80px;
grid-gap: 2rem;
justify-content: space-around;
align-content: space-between;
}
```

The `space-around` property means that the free space is distributed on each side of the items of the grid, in this particular case on the horizontal axis.

The `space-between` on the other hand, means that the available free space is distributed between the items of the grid, in this case on the vertical axis.

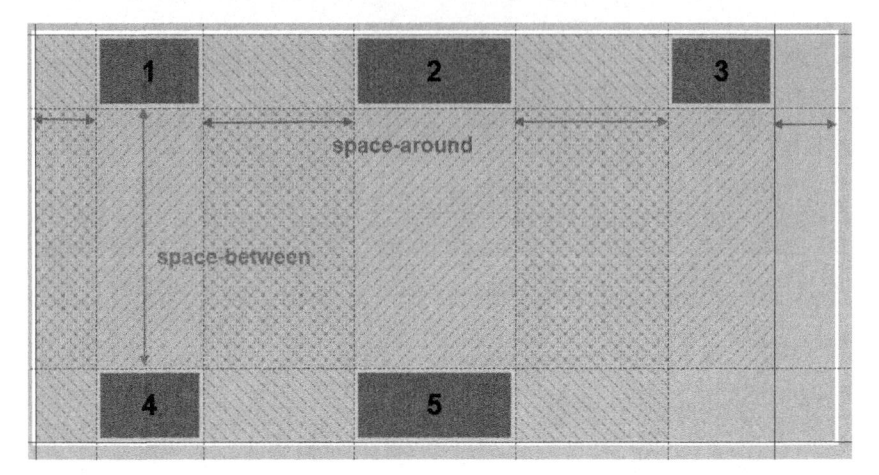

Notice also, that the gap between columns and rows does not correspond to the declared value anymore. Furthermore, items will also increase their size, if they are spanned across multiple tracks.

- Edit the CSS code once again:

```
.container {
display: grid;
border: 4px solid #fff;
width: 900px;
height: 450px;
grid-template-columns: 120px 180px 120px;
grid-template-rows: 80px 80px;
grid-gap: 2rem;
justify-content: space-evenly;
```

```
align-content: space-evenly;
}
```

The `space-evenly` property distributes the available space evenly around all grid items, including all the ends i.e. up, down, and on both sides of the grid.

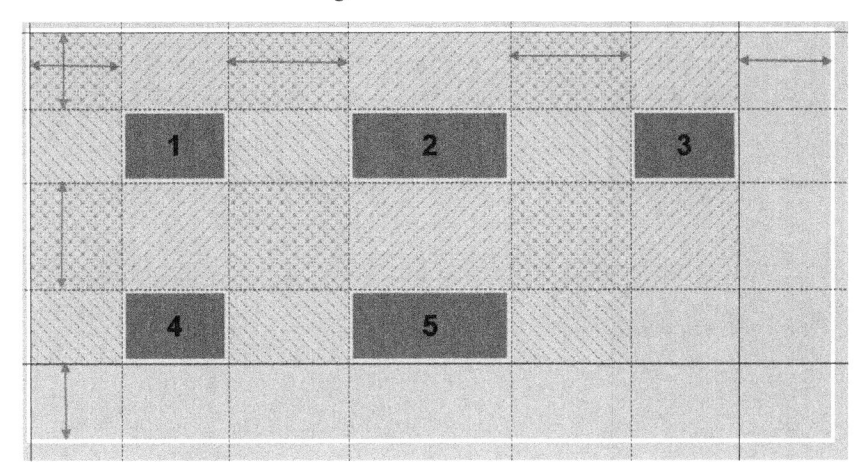

The space between the column track 1 and the column track 2 is the same as the space between the column track 1 and the left border of the grid container plus the column gap. The same applies for row tracks.

Time for you to experiment with this acquired knowledge. Build a grid with multiple columns and rows and span some of the items inside that grid. After that, test the justify-content and align-content properties. Make sure that the size of the grid container is larger than the size of the grid itself.

CHAPTER 18.

HOW TO NEST GRIDS

In the last chapter of the book, let's look at a really cool CSS Grid trick.

It is possible to turn a grid item into a grid itself, and that way, we nest a grid inside another grid. With this approach, you can break the design into different parts and lay out each one of them individually.

This will provide you with the required flexibility when converting your designs to HTML and CSS. This chapter will explain how to build nested grids.

CREATE THE HTML AND CSS

The code for this chapter is online at Github: https://github.com/OSTraining/cssgrid/tree/master/nesting.

- Create a folder called /nesting/.
- Create an HTML file called nesting.html inside the folder.
- Enter this code:

```
<html>

<head>
```

```
<link         rel="stylesheet"         type="text/css" 
href="nesting.css">
</head>

<body>

<div class="container"></div>
<div class="item item1">1</div>
<div class="item item2">2</div>
<div class="item item3">
<div class="subitem item4">4</div>
<div class="subitem item5">5</div>
</div>
<div class="item item6">6</div>
</div>

</body>

</html>
```

This layout is a container with four child Items: 1, 2, 3, and 6.

Item 3 contains two additional "subitems": 4 and 5.

Now we'll apply some basic styling to the items and subitems, in order to be able to differentiate them.

- Create a CSS file called nesting.css.
- Add the following styles:

```
/* GLOBAL STYLES */
* {
box-sizing: border-box;
}

body {
background-color: #AAA;
```

```
margin: 50px;
}

/* Each item in the grid contains numbers */
.item {
border: 5px solid #87b5ff;
border-radius: 3px;
font-family: sans-serif;
font-size: 1.5rem;
font-weight: bold;
background-color: #1c57b5;
}

.subitem {
background-color: #fdfa4e;
border: 3px solid #d32121;
}
```

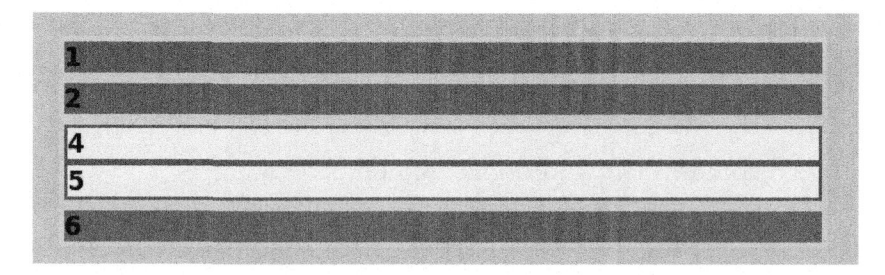

CREATE THE CSS GRID

Our grid will have two columns and a gap between items of 1rem: approximately 16px on a desktop screen.

- Add this CSS code:

```
/* CSS GRID STYLES */
.container {
display: grid;
grid-template-columns: repeat(2, 1fr);
```

```
grid-gap: 1rem;
}
```

At the very beginning of this book, we saw that grid items have to be direct children of the main grid container. Items 4 and 5 won't inherit the grid item condition of their parent element, which in this case is Item 3.

However, we can display Item 3 as a grid container itself. When we do this, we convert Items 4 and 5 into grid items, in order to lay them out inside their containing element.

NESTING A GRID INSIDE ANOTHER GRID

- Edit the CSS file once again and add this code:

```
.item3 {
display: grid;
grid-template-columns: repeat(2, 1fr);
grid-gap: 0.5em;
}
```

Now Item 3 is a grid item and also a grid container. The items inside it have turned into grid items too.

If you open the grid inspector in Firefox, you will have the option to select either of the grids on the page.

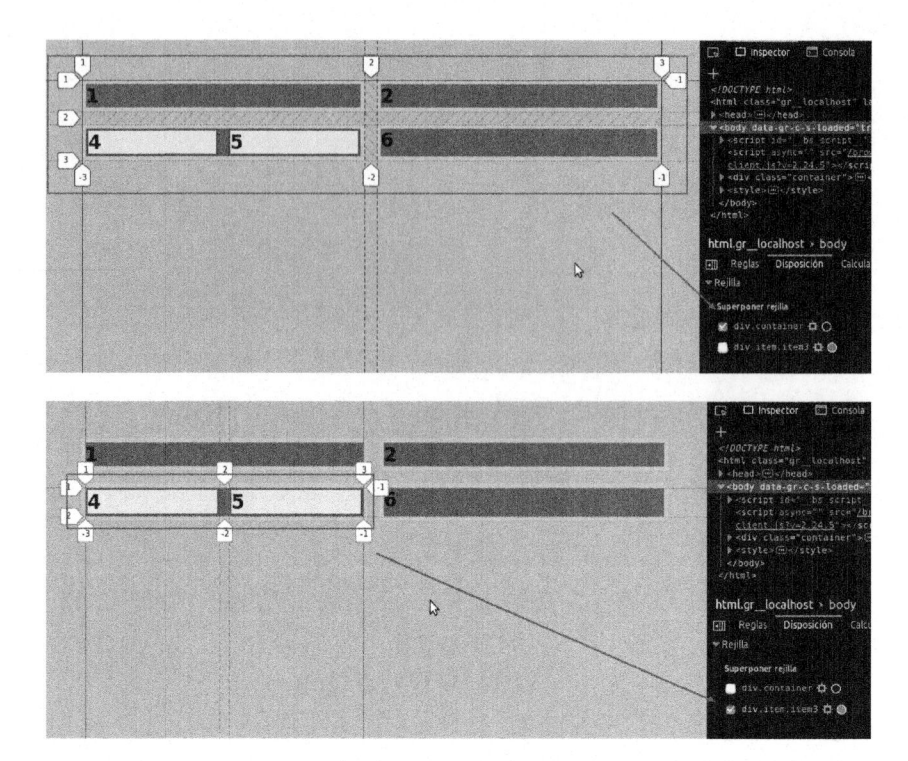

With CSS Grid, it is possible to nest grids inside other grids by converting grid items into grid containers.

This gives developers more freedom when coding a design into HTML and CSS and increases your productivity during the layout process of design mockups.